364
N213

WITHDRAWN

W9-BRK-715

Social Work Practice and Social Justice

Third NASW Professional Symposium

Selected papers
Third NASW Professional Symposium
on Social Work Practice and Social
Justice, November 26–29, 1972,
New Orleans, Louisiana

Bernard Ross and Charles Shireman, editors

The Library
Saint Francis College
Fort Wayne, Indiana 46808

NATIONAL ASSOCIATION OF SOCIAL WORKERS
1425 H Street NW
Washington, D.C. 20005

84-1677

Copyright © 1973 by the National Association of Social Workers, Inc.

International Standard Book No.: 0-87101-058-X

Library of Congress Catalog Card No.: 73-82752

Printed in the U.S.A.

 3

Contents

Contributors

Positions at the time of the symposium (November 1972)

DORENE A. BUCKLES, MSW, Social Worker, Purdy Treatment Center, Gig Harbor, Washington

LELA B. COSTIN, MSW, Professor of Social Work, Jane Addams Graduate School of Social Work, University of Illinois, Urbana-Champaign

BESS DANA, MSSA, Associate Professor and Director, Office of Education, Department of Community Medicine, Mount Sinai School of Medicine, New York, New York

DAVID FOGEL, D. Crim., Commissioner, State Department of Corrections, St. Paul, Minnesota

MITCHELL I. GINSBERG, Dean, School of Social Work, Columbia University, New York, New York, and President, National Association of Social Workers

JAMES A. GOODMAN, Ph.D., Director, Division of Special Mental Health Programs, National Institute of Mental Health, Rockville, Maryland

BERNICE C. HARPER, MSW, MSPH, Chief, Office of Long-Term Care Services, Division of Health Care Services, Community Health Service, U.S. Department of Health, Education, and Welfare, Rockville, Maryland

BARBARA KENT, BS, graduate student, Wayne State University, School of Social Work, Detroit, Michigan

MARY ANN LaFAZIA, BA, student, Graduate School of Social Work, University of Washington, Seattle

IRVING PILIAVIN, DSW, Professor, School of Social Work, University of Wisconsin, Madison

ELLEN RYAN REST, MA, Research Assistant, Probation Officer—Case Aid Project, U.S. Probation Office and Center for Studies in Criminal Justice, School of Law, University of Chicago, Chicago, Illinois

BERNARD ROSS, Ph.D., Dean, Graduate School of Social Work and Social Work Research, Bryn Mawr College, Bryn Mawr, Pennsylvania

LOUIS SCHNEIDERMAN, MSW, Assistant Professor, Graduate School of Social Work and Social Research, Bryn Mawr College, Bryn Mawr, Pennsylvania

CHARLES SHIREMAN, Ph.D., Professor and Dean of Students, School of Social Service Administration, University of Chicago, Chicago, Illinois

JEFFREY R. SOLOMON, Consultant, U.S. Department of Health, Education, and Welfare; and President, Social Consult, Inc., New York, New York

KURT SPITZER, MSW, Associate Professor and Chairman, Social Work Practice Program, Wayne State University, School of Social Work, Detroit, Michigan

RONALD I. WEINER, MSW, Assistant Professor and Director, Community and Clinical Programs, Center for the Administration of Justice, American University, Washington, D.C.

BETTI WHALEY, Director, Community Development Department, National Urban League, New York, New York

ESSEY WOLFROM, MSW, Director, Work/Training Release Program, Purdy Treatment Center, Gig Harbor, Washington

Foreword

CAN YOU, as an individual personality, obtain equity and rational response from the web of social systems in which you are enmeshed? Can we, as practitioners of applied behavioral sciences, contribute to systems change to create equity and rationality of response to each human entity?

Social Work Practice and Social Justice provides extracts from the wisdom of the social work profession to clarify the individual social dialectic. Selected from the contributions to the Third NASW Professional Symposium held in November 1972 in New Orleans, this volume concerns itself largely with the juvenile and adult justice system. Although the symposium also examined health (including mental health), income maintenance, and education systems for their social justice implications, the overwhelming deficiencies of the juvenile and adult justice systems dictated this volume's emphasis for social workers.

The treatment of "the least of these" has always been the measure of a society's social justice and also has been the basis of the need for a social work profession. Critical examination of societal successes and failures tends to sharpen practice methodology and deepen professional purpose. Hopefully this publication will stimulate increased social work attention to the subculture of our wretched and oppressed.

This volume does not record a meeting or delineate the state of a profession. In that respect, it departs from the outcomes of its forebears, two prior NASW professional symposia. *Human Services and Social Work Responsibility*, the product of the 1968 NASW symposium in San Francisco, provides a panorama of the practice context of that time. It demonstrates the necessary integration of direct practice and policy. *Trends in Social Work Practice and Knowledge* presented the text or abstract of virtually every paper presented in the first NASW national symposium of 1965 in Atlantic City.

The selectivity reflected in the contents of *Social Work Practice and Social Justice* parallels the increasing maturity of the social work profession and its organizational expression, NASW, to focus on key or priority areas of practice in order to fix responsibility and initiate action that will achieve tangible outcomes. Hopefully, its readers will catalyze this book's ideas into their own practice and personal responsibility.

CHAUNCEY A. ALEXANDER
Executive Director
National Association of Social Workers

Preface

FUNDAMENTAL TO SOCIAL WORK or any other profession is a system of values that gives purpose and direction to the profession's technology. The value system of social work is based on the dignity and worth of the person—the right of each individual to the fullest self-determination possible in a world where others have the same right.

The profession must never cease to ask how its value system is actually being implemented by current technology. Some concrete answers to this question were given at the Third National NASW Symposium held in New Orleans, Louisiana, November 26–29, 1972. The Symposium focused on social work's engagement with four client groups that are often assigned "handicapped" status and dealt with as second-class citizens. These groups are the "poor" served by the income maintenance system, the "patients" of health and mental health services, the "pupils" of public education, and the "prisoners" and others drawn into juvenile and criminal justice systems. Essentially, the central question the Symposium posed was: How can our commitment to the fundamental dignity of the individual provide standardized, competent, responsible practice?

The articles in this book are not intended to provide all the answers to that question, but only to illustrate just how critical the question is in social work today. It seemed to the editors that many of the problems of social justice are at their starkest in the juvenile and criminal justice system, and so this book includes several selections in that area. The other practice arenas discussed at the Symposium are certainly of equal importance, but social work's operational definitions of its convictions about the nature of man and the proper relationship between man and the social order transcend the lines among fields of practice. These lines largely reflect the concerns of service delivery systems at a particular juncture in history, but the problems of social justice pervade all fields of practice and reflect the concerns of the larger society.

Many people shared in the making of this book. The editors wish to acknowledge the contributions of a few of them here. The creative labor of the Symposium planning committee, including Margaret Campbell, Lewis W. Carr, Pauline Coggs, and Jessie P. Dowling, made not only the book but the Symposium possible. Ms. Dowling and Ms. Edwina Leon participated on the book committee, which developed the book's essential framework and assisted in selecting the papers. The contributions of Carolyn Nesbitt, staff associate for continuing education, NASW, are particularly appreciated. Ms. Nesbitt's energy and creativity are largely responsible for weaving the efforts of all of us into a meaningful enterprise. Particular thanks are due to Chauncey Alexander, executive director, NASW, whose confidence and vision encouraged us during the early and lonely days of planning. As editors, we are deeply grateful for the spirit and dedication and professional competence of Beatrice Saunders, director, department of publications, NASW. Finally, we thank those creative colleagues who contributed so many fine professional papers to the Symposium and especially those whose work is the contents of this book.

1

Barriers to Social Justice

Lela B. Costin,

Bernice C. Harper,

Irving Piliavin,

Betti Whaley

CERTAIN structural barriers in our society continue to obstruct social justice for the general population. It is a tragic fact in this latter part of the twentieth century that human development is not a cornerstone of the national concern. The strongest power interests in this country are not working to conserve and enhance human resources, and the essential needs of the citizenry claim only minor attention. The resultant burden of social injustice affects all citizens, but falls most heavily on the low-income and minority groups.

The lack of a national social policy in relation to human need is evident all around. A few examples may be cited: the high rates of unemployment and underemployment; the lack of marketable skills among many low-income persons and among growing numbers of young people despite the generally high level of education in this country; the continuing, active, overt discrimination by employers in matters of race, ethnic origin, sex, and age; a shortage of moderate- and low-income housing and the appalling persistence of dilapidated, overcrowded, and unsafe slum dwellings; the failure of government to deal with the economic crisis of the cities; the increasing distance between high- and low-income persons, leading the nation further into a system of two Americas—the privileged and the underprivileged; the shameful neglect of the aging; and the lack of easily available social services—"social utilities"—to prevent the onset of serious individual and family problems. The social work profession shares responsibility for these lacks in national social policy. Regrettably, the profession has not consistently and effectively communicated to government the idea that national strength and vitality can be obtained by pursuing a policy of human development.

STRUCTURAL BARRIERS

In addition to the barriers within society generally, there are structural barriers to social justice within each of the four major social welfare systems—income maintenance, juvenile and criminal justice, health care, and public education. Multiple and sometimes contradictory societal goals characterize each system. Some of these goals are made explicit and are commonly supported. Others are equally present and active but not openly espoused. Yet it is these less acknowledged goals that adversely affect the client population and act to conserve the existing social order.

Approved and openly stated goals are familiar: to make it possible for mothers of dependent children to maintain their homes in decency and health and to rear their children according to their own beliefs and family life-styles; to extend to all individuals and families the health care that will enable them to utilize the strengths which come from vigorous physical and mental health; to ensure to each person accused of crime the protections inherent in due process of law and to provide rehabilitation programs for offenders; to facilitate and guide the process of education, and to provide equal educational opportunity to all; to indoctrinate the child into the life of the society and the uses of the instrumentalities of civilization. These are the beneficent goals of the four systems; yet in each, the dominant forces of the time impose other, conservative goals and purposes that act as inequitable measures of social control.

As examples consider the following:

1. Despite significant gains during the 1960s in attention to the legal rights of low-income persons, law enforcement continues to serve principally as a means of social control of the underprivileged. Punishment, not rehabilitation or opportunity, is the dominant form of treat-

ment, and due process of law is still an elusive protection for many who are accused of crime.

2. The unreliable and inadequate income provided by public assistance and the system's punitive eligibility policies confine parents and their dependent children to a narrow, restricted environment and offer them no opportunities to redirect the course of their lives and thus alter their social status.

3. Services to enhance physical and mental health are absent in the lives of large numbers of citizens. Many people know only emergency health care, given when the inadequate health care system of this country can no longer ignore their conditions. Since they receive only partial and temporary attention to their health needs, their confinement in an oppressed and neglected social status is reinforced.

4. The present system of public education also serves in a variety of ways the less openly acknowledged purposes of social control. Through tests, curricular tracking, judgments about pupil behavior, and other means, the school sorts out and distributes pupils according to age, sex, race, and fitness for certain occupations and societal positions, but the process is not the same for all groups. The schools frequently classify children and young persons for failure as they persuade them to see themselves as the school defines them.

Contradictions in Values

Underlying these manifest and latent goals are contradictions in the values of American society. Consider the system of income security in this country. On the one hand is the belief that the United States is a family-centered society in which the child occupies a central place, and that a family's income security has a fundamental relationship to the welfare of the children. Consequently, citizens generally subscribe to the premise that income provided by society is essential in situations of poverty as a means of conserving the human resources on which the nation's future depends.

In contrast, outmoded attitudes and opinions toward the poor continue to retard progress in ending poverty. These restrictive views generally hold that it is the nature of the poor to be poor, that they have particular characteristics which predispose them to poverty and preclude effective societal remedies. The background of these contradictory societal values in relation to income and social status can be seen in the relatively recent legislative and political history of the Social Security Act. The Social Security Act was not (and is not now) a comprehensive approach to the problems of economic security. It was instead a collection of separate and limited remedies directed toward special categories of the population. Further, children's concerns were not a part of the charge to the Committee on Economic Security of 1934 even though today mothers and their dependent children make up the largest group on public assistance. Such a frame of reference ignores the poverty-inducing impact of a set of environmental circumstances or forces over which an individual has little or no control.

Contradictions in values and commitment to the client group also underlie goals in the delivery of health services. On the one hand is the conviction that health care is an essential component of an individual's capacity for a full life and is a basic right for all Americans, not just an expensive privilege for the few. Yet on the other hand the country continues to maintain a free-enterprise system of health care—one whose profits depend on illness, not on bringing people up to optimal levels of mental and physical health. As a result, too many people tend to view the crisis in health care as a crisis only for the poor, for members of minority groups, and for the aged. It is, in fact, a crisis for all Americans.

The system of criminal justice is also based on contradictions in values. In this society punishment of offenders against the law is regarded as a deterrent to crime and a basis for socialization. But certain groups also demand punishment as retribution—as a recompense for the offense. Therefore, society includes in its criminal justice system a measure of retribution to meet society's demand. But in recognition that too severe a punishment may lead to even more serious antisocial behavior, there has been a conscious effort to temper the imposition of punishment with social justice. Punishment must be fair; offenders must be treated equally—through uniform court procedures, control of length and severity of sentences, and granting of counsel.

Within this mixed system of punishment, social workers have tried to provide treatment and rehabilitation. As a consequence, they have frequently lent themselves to injustices. Their diagnostic judgments, though not supported by the findings of systematic investigations, have formed the basis for diverting some persons and keeping others in the system, for enabling some prisoners to have an early parole or to move out of institutions in other ways. But these professional judgments often invoke punishment or reward in a discriminatory fashion; all persons similarly situated are not treated equally. The prisoner who is not rewarded in this system of differential treatment can only regard his situation as being a result of discrimination.

The endorsed and unendorsed functions of public school education also rest on contradictions in societal values. For example, Americans boast that education is the means by which any individual can improve his status. Yet the facts show that other things being equal, schools tend only to bring children up to an intellectual level that will enable them to function in the same social and economic stratum as their parents. It is popular to regard public education as a channel for social change. Yet history reveals that the schools have for the most part preserved and passed on the existing system; they have not dared to try to change the social order. Our societal values state that every child has a right to achieve his full potential. Yet in the public schools arbitrary decision-making practices daily exclude children and young persons from school—for example, through suspension and practices in regard to "troublemakers," or through failure to provide appropriate educational programs for children who are emotionally disturbed, or physically or mentally handicapped, or non-English speaking. Behavioral science holds that approval and reward are appropriate reinforcements of behavior. Yet dysfunctional pupil behavior (as with dysfunctional client behavior in all four delivery systems) is reinforced by neglect, indifference, deterrence, corporal punishment, and other dehumanizing experiences.

Dichotomized Treatment Pattern

As one result of these less openly acknowledged societal goals and their underlying contradiction in values, another structural barrier to social justice emerges in the form of a dual system within each major system; that is, there is a dichotomized treatment pattern for poor persons, patients, law offenders, and school pupils. In measures to promote income security, the advantaged population is screened out of the more stringent treatment patterns in hospitals and clinics, in police stations and courts, and in public schools and into more promising programs that enhance their opportunity for optimal social functioning. The means test and the unreliable subsistence income of the parent in the Aid to Families with Dependent Children program are in direct contrast to the sanction by which high-income persons can legally evade tax payments; the barren waiting rooms and insensitive responses to human suffering which are too prevalent in public clinics and mental hospitals are stingy and dehumanizing in comparison to the facilities in which the advantaged population receives its preventive health care; the harsh experiences of the black and Puerto Rican youths in correctional institutions are in shocking contrast to private boarding schools, release with warning, probation, and payment for damages, which are available to more affluent youthful lawbreakers. And the curriculum tracking patterns in most public schools, based as they are on inadequate and unfair intelligence testing, most often result in a separate and unequal form of education for the less privileged pupils in the system.

Another structural barrier is reflected in the social distance imposed between the system serving the client and his self-image, his relationship to significant persons in his life, and his sense of home, neighborhood, and community. There are formidable contradictions in the assumption that constructive and growth-producing socialization or rehabilitation of clients can take place under conditions of complete separation from society or its concerns. Yet this kind of exile is part of the treatment in all four systems—actual separation from society, in closed institutions or in forms of rehabilitation and education that bear no relation, in the client's perception, to his "real" life and problems, and offer him association only with others of the same assigned status but no opportunity to participate in planning and directing his treatment, rehabilitation, or education.

Still another barrier to social justice is the lack of linkages between the major social welfare delivery systems. The systems tend to perceive the problems of, and center concern on, the same population groups. Yet the lack of communication between them, the failure to collaborate with each other and give attention to the needs of the client group, the absence of any effective planning for a comprehensive system of social justice have negative consequences. As a result, large numbers of juvenile offenders who leave correctional institutions never return to the public schools. Children are excluded from school because of reported mental and physical handicaps; yet the results of their neurological and pediatric examinations do not enter into the decision-making process. The lack of adequate income and other supportive services to mothers of dependent children when husbands are imprisoned and the kinds of experiences the husbands encounter as prisoners often result in estrangement between husbands and wives and between parents and children, which culminates in family breakdown when the prisoner returns to community and family.

HOW SOCIAL WORKERS CONTRIBUTE TO INJUSTICE

Has the social work profession contributed to the creation of these structural barriers to social justice or to the perpetuation of them within the four major delivery systems? The writers believe it has.

Social workers' operations seem to reflect the norms and societal goals of the system in which they work rather than the profession's values and goals. The professed goals and values of social work clash sharply with some of the major systems' goals, and yet social work intervention methods and their outcomes often do not reflect this incompatibility. Social workers, of course, are part of the general population and reflect in varying degrees the characteristics of the general culture. Are the more conservative societal values and goals still dominant among the profession's members? Have these members failed to take on the profession's values? Or do they keep them neatly compartmentalized in ways which do not interfere with their daily activities? Might this be why they have appeared to be co-opted so readily by the less openly acknowledged goals of the four systems? Do social workers note the racially segregated patterns of treatment in the major social service systems and record these only as problems for society as a whole without feeling they have any special responsibility for dealing with them? To the extent that this is so, social workers and the national professional organization toward which they look for leadership lend themselves to the maintenance of racial injustice and are guilty of discriminating against the very people they are committed to help.

Certainly it can be said that social work education has contributed to the maintenance of social injustice within these systems. It has done so by placing students and new professionals in systems that inflict dehumanizing experiences without placing on them the obligation to perform differently than have the professionals already in these systems— without teaching them how to perform so they will contribute to system change; to an improved environment; to abolition of cruelty, insensitivity, and harsh, uncaring relationships; and to development of a climate that fosters recovery, learning, rehabilitation, and constructive connections with the mainstream of society.

Social work's reluctance to give up its primary emphasis on individual pathology and rehabilitation in its treatment patterns and its tendency to ignore cultural norms and social structures have placed its members in the position of helping to perpetuate social injustice in the four systems. Other barriers to social justice include the reluctance to work in the major systems as opposed to working in the voluntary treatment sectors, and the failure to consider the impact on the client of his environment, the closed doors to opportunity, and the daily pressures that result from social conditions over which he has no control.

The social work profession has not understood the systems within which it works. There has been too little understanding of the power bases, the conflicting values, and the concomitant lack of commitment to sound public social policy. There has been far too little involvement in policy formulation within the systems and in supplying manpower trained in the methods of advocacy, social change, and social technology.

In addition, social workers have tended to support current legislation without sufficient analysis of its real purposes and possible outcomes, and without sufficient declaration of its deficiencies. For example, in the 1950s the profession did not take a strong enough stand against the Aid to Dependent Children program, nor did it counteract the expectation that the 1962 public welfare amendments could succeed despite inadequate and unreliable levels of assistance payments. This failure to identify basic social problems and to be involved in resolving them has caused the profession to lose some of its legitimacy. Neutrality has given support to the forces of conservatism.

In addition, the profession has not accounted for its services, either to the supporting public or to its membership. Perhaps social workers have been complacent about the need to do so and to justify their claim on scarce financial resources because they believe that their work does not lend itself to statistical counts and testing. Perhaps it is not in fact as readily testable as some other public services. Yet the profession must accept responsibility to devise alternative means of assembling data that will improve accountability in the giving of services. Schools of social work, in turn, must teach not only the means for more effective delivery of social services, but the means and the necessity for authentic professional accountability as well.

THE CHALLENGE TO SOCIAL WORK

How, then, can social work play an effective role in the four major social welfare delivery systems? The most urgent necessity is to begin to evolve, promulgate, and train for new models of social service delivery in each system. This implies a model of social work practice that encompasses client-treatment, system-community relations. Clear emphasis on social justice and advocacy to humanize the treatment system is essential. No matter how great their desire to be a part of the service team, social workers are not justified in protecting the system against outside criticism.

Advocacy also necessitates a readiness to allow clients a greater share in planning and directing their own treatment, rehabilitation, or education; a paternalistic system, however benign, does not assure social justice. The aim must be to prepare social workers to view the major delivery systems as vital and strategic institutions in the lives of all people, the community, and the nation. Social workers must assume leadership in aiding these systems to adapt to the special and urgent needs of their clients, particularly of those target groups who presently have least access to just treatment and who endure the most pressing societal problems. They cannot continue to lend themselves to the latent functions of bureaucracies and to the continuation of outmoded systems.

If social workers are to fill a significant role in a changing society, they must develop a fuller understanding of their own actions and of the social changes and processes going on in all sectors of our national life. They must face the fact that they will continue to encounter stress and tension in the systems in which they work; that a broad expertise is required; and that uncertainty in the systems and in their roles will continue. The challenge is to utilize the opportunities inherent in that uncertainty.

2

The Justice System of the Future

Charles Shireman

THE ANCIENT Chinese are said to have used this curse: "May you live in interesting times!" Social workers involved in the juvenile and criminal justice system of today are living in all too interesting times. A tide of change seems to be sweeping away the certainties on which they have based their careers. Applications of research methods and of increasingly precise measurement instruments have produced doubt and disillusionment rather than confirmation and sureness. Social workers in corrections are no longer confident even of the essential justice of the criminal justice system. Their diagnoses are impressive but seem to lead to disappointingly little treatment. At the same time, "security" institutions are becoming frighteningly insecure. What took place at Attica (N.Y.) State Prison in 1972 was, with the exception of the Indian wars of the last century, the bloodiest one-day confrontation among Americans since the Civil War.

For what comfort it may bring, social workers are not alone. All disciplines go through recurring periods of breaking up long-dominant systems of knowledge and values and replacing them with new ones. This is the process of growth and change. Such experiences extend to the physical as well as the social sciences. Indeed, we may achieve a clearer perspective by noting the similarities between our position today and that of one of the physical sciences—astronomy—at another turning point of history.

The accepted theory of astronomy in the early seventeenth century was sophisticated, internally consistent, and intellectually satisfying. Its elaborate structures showed with reassuring exactitude how the sun, the planets, and the stars all orbited around man's home—Earth, the center of the universe. But the coming of the telescope and the resultant, more precise observations of Galileo and others shattered this comfortable state of affairs. The new data raised disquieting new questions instead of providing answers. Reluctantly, scientists began to see that no adjustment of the accepted framework would enable it to accommodate the new data, and that only a fundamentally different framework, the one proposed by Copernicus, would explain all the facts. This was a difficult shift to make because it meant giving up man's position at the center of the universe, but what made it harder was that no smooth transition from one stage of understanding to the next was possible. All at once science had to adopt a whole new way of looking at things.[1]

Today criminological and correctional practice and theory are at a point analogous to pre-Copernican astronomy. For almost two centuries we have been relatively satisfied with the human relations concepts on which the criminal justice system rested. But in the past few years things have gone seriously awry. Previous lines of thought now seem to produce savage violence rather than tranquil progress, disquieting doubts and despair rather than certainty. It becomes ever more clear that what is needed are new perceptions of the relationship between the offender and the social order—whole new ways of looking at the problem.

PREVIOUS CONCEPTIONS

This is not the first time that criminal justice has reached such a turning point. Current patterns of juvenile and criminal justice probably represent a final flowering of perceptions of the nature of man and of the relationships between man—including criminal man—and society that emerged in the late eighteenth and early nineteenth centuries. Before then, persons labeled "criminal" were considered to be unnatural beings, perhaps possessed by devils, less than human. Crimes were ill defined, and the state exercised arbitrary powers to convict and punish for a wide variety of behaviors now considered matters of private conscience. There was a bewildering array of capital offenses, and punishment ranged from burning alive to mutilation, whipping, branding, and the pillory. All this seemed proper to rational, thoughtful, and decent men.

There came a time when these patterns of belief and action no longer seemed to meet the needs of new generations. The revolutionary tide of the era brought with it ideas irreconcilable with then-current criminological doctrine and practice. The Declaration of Independence in America and the Declaration of the Rights of Man in France set the stage for new perceptions of the nature of man and of the criminal. These brought in their wake new conceptions of the nature of criminal justice based on liberal thought and the new humanitarianism.

Humanitarianism

Among the earliest and most enduring fruits of this new stream of humanitarian thought was a radical American invention, the prison, then termed the penitentiary. The penitentiary was to be a place of true penitence and a pathway back to the ways of God and man. It was conceived in Pennsylvania by the most dedicated and creative humanitarians of the day—the Quakers. Individual cells, decent food and clothing, and religious counsel were thought by men of good will to represent the outstretched hand of Christian charity. This attitude illustrates the new perception of the offender. The criminal, although one with mankind, had gone astray. There was something wrong within his heart and soul, he was sick and misguided. Thus he was dangerous to other men and must be incarcerated or "incapacitated" so he could harm no one until he was "cured." Like the physically ill, he was at the same time to be pitied, done to, done for, and "changed" so that he would become penitent and wish to return to a more acceptable way of life.

Here, then, was the dawn of what one thoughtful scholar has termed "the era of the rehabilitative ideal." The needed and inevitable new way of looking at things had emerged. Human behavior came to be seen as the natural result of antecedent causes, which could be discovered and understood. As a result of such understanding, human conduct could be controlled, and thus the treatment of the offender should have a therapeutic function. For the first time in history rehabilitation became a major theme in society's verbalizations of its motivations with respect to the offender.

The last century and a half has in many respects been a period of visible achievement. It has ushered in the concept of returning the offender to the community with the helping services of probation and parole. It has brought the juvenile court, prison classification, separate facilities for juveniles and females, and merit-system employment of correctional staff. Whole new professional helping services have been provided by the chaplain, the educator, the vocational instructor, the social worker, the psychiatrist, and even the plastic surgeon. In the institution "custody" remains, perhaps, the dominant theme, but "treatment" jockeys with it for power, not always unavailingly. The year 1972 *may* have seen in the United States the elimination of that remnant of barbarism, capital punishment.

FAILURES

These have been real advances, but the past few years have also brought widespread fears that many of the fruits of the reform have been bitter. The major failure, of course, has been the prison. In spite of vaunted reforms, recurring waves of prison violence have occurred, with accelerated use of deadly force. The modern prison has been termed a "warehouse of degradation" by a former attorney general of the United States. It is in recent years seen with increasing clarity as the product of a penal policy that "for the most part [is] a policy of isolation and punishment, accompanied by the rhetoric of rehabilitation, which results in chronic underfinancing, inadequate staffing, deflected sexuality, and general lack of resources and poverty of imagination." [2]

What is even more disillusioning is that the failures extend beyond the prison. It seems probable that the more advanced helping services do help some offenders, but they may be actually harmful to others. So unimpressive have their success rates generally been that sober scholars advance persuasive theories to the effect that the least amount of treatment may be the best treatment for most offenders, and that the further the individual goes through the correctional systems the less are his chances of being "corrected." Data permitting informed evaluation of helping efforts are seldom collected, but such as are available are hardly reassuring. For example, one too-little-known study carried out by the District of Columbia Corrections Department traced the correctional histories of a random sample of twenty-five young men released from the District of Columbia Youth Center.[3] The median age of these young men was 26. Their correctional records averaged 9 years and included 25 correctional actions and services, ranging from juvenile arrest to prison terms. The "rehabilitative" care given each of them had included an average of 32 months in the District of Columbia Youth Center, 8½ months in federal reformatories, 4½ months in jail, 23 months on parole, 2 months on adult probation, 16 months in welfare institutions, 22 months in foster homes, and 6 months on juvenile probation. Thus far, the median cost of their correctional care had been $31,000 per person. And these calculations were made as they were being released for another ride on the merry-go-round!

Doubts of the justice of the criminal justice system and of the ability of the correctional programs to do much "correcting" are being voiced with ever increasing insistency. These doubts prompt even greater disquietude and more searching questions. From what philosophical base *should* one develop a juvenile and criminal justice system? With what conception of the nature of the relationship between the offender and society? Or, for that matter, with what conviction about the relationship between man and man?

ILLUSIONS

A number of postulates that have until now been cherished and upon which major aspects of the criminal justice system have been based are now being recognized as illusions. Together, these illusions have created a mythology that has been mistaken for reality to such a degree as to make rational policy development in criminal justice impossible. Among the key elements of this illusory system the following must be included.

Criminal Justice Has Been Achieved

Fundamental fairness and the absence of capricious abuse of the enormous power of the state would seem to be essential elements of any program designed to rehabilitate offenders. Indeed, recent years have brought increasing attention to the need for procedural fairness in society's confrontation with the offender. Decisions in the Mapp, Gideon, Miranda, Escobedo, and Gault cases, for example, are among the system's proudest accomplishments. But have these decisions in favor of due process truly been major victories or are they more accurately perceived as mere skirmishes in the battle for criminal justice? Indeed, one might argue that preoccupation with the struggle for due process at and immediately preceding the trial level may have served as a diversion from an attack on the major criminal and social justice problems of the day. Consider a bill of particulars such as the following:

1. Most social scientists, most lawyers in their reflective moods, and surely just about all defendants know it is cruel nonsense to believe the assumption that the offender is solely responsible for his behavior and that there is justice in the way the state goes about fixing his guilt for such behavior. We know something today of the origins of

behavior. Social workers in particular know that the proper target for intervention is the transactional field composed of both individual personality and social environment. We know the manner in which the sins and sicknesses within the social order contribute to the lesser crimes of the individual. But, we say, we have jurisdiction over the individual offender, not over the long life experience that crippled him, not over the social problem that channeled his rage. Thus we bring him alone—not the horrible injustice that created him—before the bar of justice. It is he alone who must pay for the sins of mankind. This is criminal justice?

2. The offender who is subjected to penal sanctions is perfectly aware that he is unfortunate in being selected for such dubious distinction from an enormous number of offenders, many or most of whom may have committed more serious offenses than his. The process whereby he is selected for punishment will inevitably seem to him to be so wildly capricious as to bear not the slightest relationship to justice. To begin with, cultural mores define the types of behavior that are defined as crimes. Cultural mores also assure that only in rare instances will certain types of crime even be subject to law enforcement. As a soul-searching, deeply moving publication of the American Friends Service Committee notes:

> We measure crime, and thereby define both the nature of the problem and the image we form of the criminal, by counting complaints, arrests, or convictions and classifying the suspected or known violators by race, age, census tract, or socioeconomic class. From this we draw the image of the typical criminal—urban, young, poor, black. But if we applied the same counting standards to polluters, price fixers, deceptive advertisers, manufacturers of dangerous merchandise, landlords of substandard housing, minimum wage cheaters, or other known violators of similar criminal laws, we would have a very different picture. Unbiased statistics on the incidence of crime would probably show that the proportion of criminals in various segments of a population increases with wealth and power, and it seems certain that the loss caused to victims of such "rich" crime far exceeds that of the usual lower class criminality. . . .
>
> Were our convicted thieves actually representative of the population that illicitly deprives other people of their money, then our criminologists might be pouring onto Madison Avenue the way they now analyze and reanalyze the ghetto, our psychologists would be flipping those ink blots in an attempt to determine why the affluent always want more, and in our prisons the study. of

business ethics might replace the course on auto mechanics. [Our policies] further distort the vision of those who can always see black crime in the ghetto but never white crime in Scarsdale or Palo Alto.[4]

3.   Even if only the "traditional" crimes against property and of violence of the sort commonly reported to police are considered, a large element of chance—or of glaringly obvious bias—operates in the selection of offenders for the imposition of sanctions. Precise documentation is difficult, but evidence indicates that of every hundred crimes committed, less than fifty are reported to the police. Of these only twelve result in arrest, which leads to six convictions, and to a screened-out two offenders being sent to prison. The two who do go to prison are likely to be poor and either young or members of a minority group— those who are least able to defend themselves and to propose attractive alternatives to correctional care. The whole process is made even more irrational by the fact that in a large proportion of cases, such convictions as are made, result from the ubiquitous plea-bargaining that renders highly improbable conviction for an offense that even approximately resembles the actual violative behavior of the accused.

What is the value to the practitioner of these abstract meditations on the selective process in criminal justice? That is easy. Biased selection from the offender population leads to biased perceptions of the criminal. He is of a different order—"sick" or "perverted," not quite on par with other humans. And such biased perceptions produce distorted and shabby treatment. Further, such biases facilitate the adoption of rationalizations for shabby treatment—rationalizations in the form of illusions such as those that follow.

The Rhetoric of Rehabilitation

From the first step taken toward modern corrections—the founding of what was to become the present prison system—rehabilitative treatment has been more rhetoric than reality. The idealized new penitentiary, with its emphasis on solitary meditation as a pathway to redemption, did more to drive inmates insane than to redeem them. The use of rhetoric of rehabilitation still masks older, more savage practices.

Consider, for example, a feature of most juvenile correctional institutions, the security or isolation unit. Most large institutions have them. Most probably need them as a means of temporary protective care of youngsters undergoing emotional explosions during which they might be destructive of themselves or others. All that these units are is cell blocks. But in institution after institution how are they officially labeled?

"Intensive treatment units" or "treatment cottages" or "meditation units." How much sense does this make unless we realize the degree to which rhetoric masks more ancient attitudes of fear and hatred of the offender?

Consider the reality of our expectations of probation and parole as treatment services. Since at least the 1920s social workers have been striving in this country for "reasonable" caseloads. For at least that long, we have spoken of the "fifty-unit caseload" as the minimum standard toward which we should strive. We rarely achieve this standard, but we still speak of it as our reasonable goal. Seldom do we step back and view objectively what the accomplishment of such a goal would mean. For example, it would obviously mean the availability on the part of the supervising probation or parole officer of an average of about three hours a month for all work in connection with each case. Not impressive? Well, then, consider that by the time allowance is made for travel, dictation, waiting for the court, collateral call time, supervisory interviews, and a number of other demands, it is unlikely that the officer will have more than forty-five minutes per month for in-person contact with a probationer or parolee. How much rehabilitative treatment does this allow?

The illusion of treatment probably is a major negative factor. The youthful offender, for example, recidivates "in spite of all the help he was given." The only possible conclusion must be that he is so intractable as to be "untreatable" or that treatment must be impossible—when the substance of treatment was never present behind the façade.

All Offenders Can Be Changed

Fundamental to the thinking of many pursuers of the rehabilitative ideal is the belief that all, or almost all, offenders need and will respond to rehabilitative efforts if such efforts are sufficiently massive and persistent. People will change; human behavior, ultimately, is pliable, it is assumed. The relative lack of success of these efforts to date is the remediable result either of inadequate investment or of inadequate will. But doubts are beginning to arise. In recent years discouraging results have been reported from an array of projects that would seem to have fairly tested various ways of "treating" all comers. Small caseloads, group counseling, psychiatric treatment, intensive remedial or vocational education, early release to halfway houses or other treatment, "token economies," "guided group interaction"—all have been tested to at least some degree. Many of these treatment models seem to help some offenders, but it also appears that they are unable to help many others and may be actually harmful to some. The margin that any of them has clearly demonstrated over no treatment at all is not dramatic. Indeed, it is becoming increasingly apparent that the profession must confront the uncomfortable possibility that the modification of basic values and of personality traits is harder than has been thought. The awesome goal of changing human beings *is* awesome. For many, it may be unattainable by any method practically or ethically available.

The illusions just discussed are rarely tested, however. In particular, it seldom occurs to us to collect data systematically as to how the "treated" assess these assumptions. We seem to assume that they do not know what their "real" problems are, and that they are incapable of judging or of reporting whether they have been helped. Does this, perhaps, suggest to social work, a profession dedicated to the necessity of a "partnership in problem-solving," some of the elements of the new way of looking at things that must emerge?

In the meantime, these illusions lead us to assign most offenders to programs of active intervention in their lives. The result is the choking of programs with large numbers of individuals who do not need, do not want, and cannot use the sort of relationship-and-communication-based treatment that is the basis for most probation or parole services. Only if the illusory system is dispelled will we be able to experiment with differential diagnoses that will lead to prescriptive choices among treatment: environmental intervention, "brokerage" of other available services, advocacy on behalf of clients, or various forms of relationship-based counseling. Social workers are still in the early stages of gaining the ability to treat prescriptively, but imaginative efforts are being made. Notable among these is the diagnostic typology of California's Community Treatment Project.[5] Somewhat more parsimonious theoretically and probably pointing one way ahead would be the "task-centered casework" line of development, with its focus on client-perceived and verbalized problems, newly conceptualized by Reid and Epstein.[6]

THE FUTURE SYSTEM: AREAS FOR REFORM

The injustices and the myths of contemporary practice are becoming more and more widely recognized. Although the nature of the juvenile and criminal judicial system of the future is not clear, certain outlines, still hazy as to detail, are emerging. The shape of many of them is almost certainly congruent with the essential framework of prescriptions long promulgated, if not always practiced, by social workers. The present challenge to social work is to translate its prescriptions into practice harmonious with current and future needs.

There is one sure way of cutting the crime rate in half; reducing much of the overload on law enforcement, courts, and jails; and sparing a large proportion of those presently labeled as "offenders" the pain, frustration, and criminogenic influence of involvement with the criminal justice system at its worst. That is to remove from the criminal law those behaviors offensive to our sense of propriety but otherwise harmful only to the perpetrator—the so-called crimes without victims. The fundamental purposes of the criminal law are to protect persons and property and to guard against the exploitation of the young or others who require special protection. As Morris and Hawkins state:

> In this country we have a highly moralistic criminal law and a long tradition of using it as an instrument for coercing men toward virtue. It is a singularly inept instrument for that purpose. It is also an unduly costly one both in terms of harm done and in terms of the neglect of the proper task of law enforcement. . . . It is based on an exaggerated conception of the capacity of the criminal law to influence men. We incur enormous collateral disadvantage costs for that exaggeration and we overload our criminal justice system to a degree which renders it grossly defective as a means of protection in the areas where we really need protection—from violence, incursions into our homes, and depredations of our property.[7]

Victimless crimes that should be removed from criminal law include drunkenness, drug use (though the sale of some drugs other than by prescription would still be a criminal act), gambling, much disorderly conduct and vagrancy, sexual behavior between consenting adults in private, and much juvenile delinquency. Together, the adult crimes listed account for almost half of the some eight million arrests in 1971. Drunkenness alone contributed some two million arrests, thus enormously overloading the misdemeanant courts and rendering much of their work futile.

This is not to say that persons involved in behavior hurtful to themselves should be denied active social concern. For example, if common drunks must be rounded up every night in certain portions of the city, do it as a social service. Provide a voluntary "drying-out and sleep-it-off" facility; or, for that matter, take them home, as the prowl car frequently does the drunk from the well-to-do residential district. But if those now involved in the violations of contemporary morality are to be served effectively, if the rehabilitative ideal is to be realized with respect to them, it must be through the extension of services offered on a voluntary basis. This will never be accomplished as long as these persons remain within the purview of the criminal law.

The Rights of Offenders

The central core of the value system of social work is its belief in the dignity of man. Social workers have long emphasized their dedication to the principle of man's right to free choice—his right to live his own life as he sees fit, so long as he does not interfere with rights of others.

However, these beliefs have not been applied to offenders. In effect, offenders have been deprived of all their rights; they have been made nonpersons at law. There was until recently, in fact, a presumption of "civil death" for the offender, and in many ways it still prevails. Under this presumption, the convicted and sentenced offender was held to have lost all civil rights and private trusts. It was considered permissible to hold him in steel and concrete cages that degraded and dehumanized him—after all, he had forfeited all membership in the human community.

Social acceptance of this position has been so broad that until recently prisoners also believed in its validity. Thus they gave that degree of tacit consent to the conditions of their care without which the administration of a community of captives is impossible. But within the past few years these basic attitudes have been reversed. It is now evident that in any situation in which there are two parties—the "keepers" and the "kept"—with all formal power is vested in the keepers, all participants will be corrupted. Concepts of the "rights of prisoners" are rapidly emerging from the crucible of prison unrest. Even more importantly, it is coming to be recognized that offenders, including prison inmates, must have the power to enforce their rights. Such realizations will inevitably presage the development of usable channels through which the kept can invoke the law and hold the keeper responsible for invasions of their rights.

The implications of such a position are manifold. As a beginning, the prisoner must have ready access to the courts. Greatly increased court surveillance to assure decent standards of prison care becomes imperative. Like it or not, social workers in corrections are seeing the beginning of the end of the judicial "hands-off" doctrine as applied to the maintenance of the basic rights of prisoners. The criminal justice system will continue to be responsible for that degree of secure care necessary to assure that the offender does not invade the rights of others. But the test of every rule, every regulation, every procedure will have to be whether it is justified by the need to retain that necessary minimal degree of control. Thus the central thrust of the system's efforts must become the creation of a situation in which the offender retains to the maximum degree his status as a dignified, self-directing human being.

Other areas that must be examined range from the prevalent petty rules regarding a prisoner's personal appearance to his right to participate in an informed way in the parole decision or personally to call legislative or other public attention to the condition of his care. And how many social workers in the correctional field have looked recently at the conditions of parole or of probation in their state? How possible is it to incarcerate the offender for technical violations, for behavior not considered violative when performed by others?

Dependence on Incarceration

In the foreseeable future, it will be necessary to detain in various degrees of isolation from the community a relatively small number of individuals who represent a threat to the security of their fellow citizens. It is naïve to assume that the present dilemma can be solved simply by eliminating prisons. But it is time to confront the fact that the correctional institution has a limited social utility. At the least, it is essential to face the implications of two related, discouraging observations now almost accepted as truisms by careful analysts of the field: (1) the correctional institution is much more likely to be criminogenic than corrective in its impact on the offender, and (2) imprisonment is enormously expensive in both human and financial terms. A number of experiments have demonstrated that there are less costly ways of dealing with offenders. For example:

1. Ten years ago the Saginaw (Michigan) project of the National Council on Crime and Delinquency demonstrated that 80 percent of felony offenders could be placed on probation without danger to the community. In just eighty-eight cases the citizens of Michigan saved over $400,000, and the recidivism rate decreased markedly.[8]
2. In New Mexico, an effective probation and parole system was instituted. As a result, the prison population was reduced from 1,500 to 800, and the proposed expenditure of $20 million for a new institution was found unwarranted.[9]
3. In the field of juvenile corrections a few experiments have been carried out in various parts of the country in which randomly selected groups of juveniles committed by courts to institutions have been retained in the community and included in a variety of community-based treatment programs. Their adjustment has been compared with that of control groups who have gone on into institutional care and then been released. These projects have varied and so have their findings. However, one common result is that, almost invariably, the youngsters retained in the community do better than those sent to institutions—and

their care costs the community far less.[10] And as the National Council on Crime and Delinquency notes:

> When the Senate Juvenile Delinquency Subcommittee held public hearings into the problem of juvenile institutions and prisons in March, 1969, administrators of juvenile programs testified that it would be better if many delinquents were never apprehended because they deteriorate rather than improve under the guardianship of the state. The public probably would receive better protection by releasing young offenders back onto the streets rather than sending them to institutions where they become more dangerous and more adept at crime.[11]

Most illusions about the rehabilitative potential of the walled institution that houses under degrading conditions as many as three thousand or more adult felons, for the most part in idleness or in meaningless activity, have by now been dispelled. It is being recognized ever more widely that it is necessary to accelerate the development of systems composed of relatively small institutions located in, and closely related to, areas from which most of the inmates are drawn, resembling as closely as possible normal residential settings, and having only a few high-security units. Eventually, if all too slowly, the present "fortress prison" will disappear.

Other inroads on the classic dependence on the institution are on the way. Among the most promising are early, gradual return to the community with the aid of furloughs, community halfway houses, educational leave, and work release programs. Massachusetts has embarked on the most exciting adventure on the correctional scene: it is closing almost all of its juvenile correctional institutions—and it has done so under the leadership of a social worker.

The Bail System

But the determination to find and use alternatives to institutions wavers. One little-taken but perfectly available opportunity for reform—in which the detrimental impact of incarceration at its worst could easily be avoided—lies in the further development of alternatives to the bail bond system.

The local jail, in which the idleness, corruption, brutality, and moral deterioration of prison life are most revealing, houses persons awaiting trial as well as those serving short sentences. In 1965 the average daily population of such institutions in the United States was over 141,000.[12]

offender and society the opportunity for treatment, assuming that both are interested in treatment.

Although not necessarily utile, an admixture of other motives—vengeance, retribution, and deterrence—seems to be present in varying degrees when incarceration is under discussion. Adherents of wider use of incarceration are hard put to make a case for the efficiency of incarceration in reducing crime. Yet it is widely held by nonadherents that some form of incarceration will probably always be required because when certain types of behavior are involved the immediate need to calm the public will take precedence over any evidence concerning its nonutility. Indeed, the credibility of other measures to deal with offenders is linked in the public's mind with the system's ability to keep the more highly visible offenders off the streets. It is, therefore, not so much a question of whether to give up incarceration as how to make it a more rational process.

Many complex problems confront correction officials in their quest for efficiency, but the most significant task is production of a comprehensive statement of what the public can expect from corrections now and what the public might expect if corrections can successfully change its fortress prison approach.

RESEARCH

It is the author's belief that the research findings of the last two decades should be accepted and a new approach developed. Two reviews of research in the field of corrections point to similar conclusions.[1]

Greenberg reviewed research on the effectiveness of penal methods. He found that such methods as warnings, intensity of probation, and use of halfway houses were no better than the usual methods of incarceration, probation, or parole; while use of fines, conjugal visits and home furloughs, and probation versus incarceration were better. In addition, he found no significant differences between the use of such innovative techniques as milieu therapy, group counseling, individual psythotherapy, casework, and development of skills and the usual methods; nor was incarceration in an open or closed institution significant. Greenberg did not include work release programs in his review because there were no published studies of them at that time.

Hood and Sparks reviewed research on the effectiveness of punishment and treatment. They concluded:

> . . . probation is likely to be at least as effective in preventing recidivism as an institutional sentence. . . . However [it] cannot be

interpreted as showing that probation is especially effective as a method of treatment.

. . . fines and discharges are much more effective than either probation or imprisonment for first offenders and recidivists of all age groups (. . . fines are especially effective for those convicted of theft). . . . It must be emphasized that this finding does not necessarily support the view that any offenders now sent to penal institutions should as a matter of policy, be dealt with by non-institutional methods instead. Such a course could itself affect the recidivism rates of these and other offenders, as well as reducing the general-preventive effect of the penal system. *Moreover, even if recidivism rates did not rise, a shift to non-institutional sentences would lead to an increased crime rate, since it would mean that some offenders now sent to institutions (and so not "at risk") for a time would instead be at liberty in the community during that time.* The social cost of these extra offenses would have to be balanced, in any policy calculation, against the excess cost of keeping the offenders in institutions rather than leaving them in the community.

Longer institutional sentences are no more effective in preventing recidivism than shorter ones.

Medium risk offenders are most likely to be affected by new penal methods. The persistent and low risk offenders are least likely to be affected. All groups are identifiable by prediction methods now in use.

It must be admitted that [many] studies . . . have negative results: that is, they reveal no significant differences between the types of treatment investigated . . . even a marginal improvement in the overall "success rate" from 60 to 70 percent, for example, would be to reduce recidivism by one-quarter; and this would be no mean achievement.[2]

In a nutshell, under present conditions, nothing much works effectively. Hood and Sparks believe that future effectiveness may lie in the direction of "new forms of treatment, for particular types of offenders," while Greenberg believes that there is

. . . a gap between theory and experiment. Most rehabilitation programs have had little or no link with any plausible theory of why convicted persons were previously involved in crime or why they might return to it. Random experimentation is not a very efficient way of generating new knowledge, as studies reported . . . prove so well.[3]

Assuming that both surveys are right, the findings would suggest the following strategy:

The greatest numbers of crimes are committed by treatable offenders who have not learned how to respond lawfully to an environment that does not give them the feeling that they have a "stake" in their society and/or enough opportunities to change their life's circumstances in a satisfactory manner. The career felons (professional, syndicate criminals), in this theory, are assumed to be least treatable. The dangerously violent are also excluded as psychiatric problems unresponsive to present correctional treatment.

It follows logically, therefore, that separate living and care programs should be provided for the psychiatric and high-risk or career felons: for the former, a concentration of psychiatric services and indeterminate sentences; for the latter, flat-time sentences in a milieu of austere but humane and reasonable constitutional care. The largest remaining group, the middle-risk group, should be engaged in a "justice model" of treatment in medium-security facilities following a diagnostic period.

THE JUSTICE MODEL

A fruitful way of teaching non-law-abiders to be law-abiding is to treat them in a lawful way. The entire correctional agency must be involved in the effort to influence these non-law-abiders by a program of teaching them lawful behavior.

The justice model would include efforts to place inmate populations and staff in a lawful and rational milieu. For example, the elements for a prison would specifically, but not exhaustively, include the following:

1. Elements of self-governance.
2. A system-wide ombudsman independent of the department of corrections.
3. A law library.
4. Legal assistance with the civil law.
5. Payment of wages at the prevailing private industry rate in the prison industries.
6. Opportunity to provide community service (a form of moral restitution).
7. Recognition of, and opportunity for, programming for different ethnic groups.
8. Due-process safeguards built into internal behavior management systems.
9. No mail censorship.

10. An extensive furlough program.

11. A contract system for parole, with objective criteria for progression through the incarceration experience.

12. Introduction of adversary and appeal procedures into the parole revocation decision-making process.

13. Open access to the correctional system for the news media.

14. Compensation for victims of crimes and restitution by offenders.

15. The right to vote for convicts (by absentee ballot) and the automatic restoration of civil rights upon parole.

Programs

Programs would include education, recreation, vocational training, and industrial work opportunities: For those who wished to receive social work, psychological, or psychiatric services, a voucher system could be provided. A separate internal police force would enforce, when necessary, the explicated norms of this new prison society. Only a small part of the staff would have police functions, the major effort being carried out by a nonuniformed counseling staff.

This model purports to turn a prison experience into one that teaches and provides opportunities for men to learn to be agents in their own lives, to use legal processes to change their condition, and to wield lawful power. Men who can negotiate their fates do not have to resort to violence as a method of achieving change.

This strategy might provide the keeper and the kept with a rationale and morality for their shared fates in a correctional agency. Considering the failure of most treatment methods within the fortress prison, the justice model holds some promise, if not to cut recidivism, then more decisively to preclude riots.

Maximum-Custody Rehabilitation Centers

Instead of the current fortress prison there should be maximum-custody rehabilitation centers in or near urban complexes. These centers would house no more than three hundred residents and should have the following characteristics:

1. There would be program units each composed of thirty to fifty residents. These units would permit staff assignments with manageable groups of residents. In addition, staff could be assigned to various units according to the skills needed in an area.

2. A core of central services would be provided, consisting of eight or ten different rehabilitation options. These options would include:

intake, diagnosis, classification; psychiatric care; treatment of high-risk career felons; vocational and academic education; treatment of chemical abuse; work and study release programs; preparole release; family treatment; conjugal visiting, and crisis short-term return to the centers.

3. The centers would be urban oriented. Offenders would have their families and friends close, and good professionals would be accessible.

4. Security would be achieved by means of sophisticated electronic and sensory devices used by the small custodial staff. The type of security housing included would depend on the classification of the residents.

5. Except for those in the psychiatric unit, there should be no full-time clinical professional staff members in state employ. (Although professionals have claimed that their presence in authoritative settings has humanized the treatment regimen, there is little evidence to support such claims. Rather it appears that their entry has cost them their identities.) If any resident wants social work, psychological, or psychiatric services, he can contract for it through a voucher system.

Despite serious efforts to diagnose quickly, classify, and place low-risk categories into a separate set of community-based rehabilitation options, there would always be a stable group in secure custody. The justice model can be used both for the all-risk type of program and for the community-based residential programs (which eventually would be the larger group). One Massachusetts social worker is already using this model in his field services operations, which have supplanted all the traditional correctional institutions for juveniles in that state. Youth advocate programs are being experimented with all over the country.

Extending Justice to the Convicted

It is sad that in our system of criminal justice we insist on the full majesty of due process for the accused until he is sentenced to an institution, and then justice is said to have been served. The penal codes require that before a criminal sanction may be imposed, the behavior of the accused must be found to have been a union of *act* and *intent*—i.e., it was volitional. This must be determined beyond reasonable doubt. Degrees of responsibility are reduced for the alleged behavior if such behavior was nonvolitional. Standards of arrest and for determining guilt are strict; the defendant is presumed innocent until his guilt is proved by the state.

This system is civilized and protects everyone from the capriciousness of constituted authority. However, once sentenced to prison, the offender is no longer treated with justice. The entire case for a justice model rests on the need to continue to engage the person in the quest for justice as he moves along the continuum from defendant to convict to parolee.

On one level there is need for a cultural reversal concerning the apparent attitude that the person convicted of a crime does not need or even deserve further doses of justice but rather, having proved himself "unworthy," is now removed from further consideration of just treatment. How else could the judicial dictum that the prisoner is a "slave of the state" have endured so long, accompanied quite appropriately by a judicial hands-off policy in relation to prison administration? In recent years it has become obvious that the hands-off policy is eroding. The time is most propitious for a reexamination of current styles and the development of a new rationale for the prison experience, leading the way toward engaging both the keeper and the kept in a manageable experience in prison. The keeper has always been at least as angry as the kept.

The justice model seeks to engage both the keeper and the kept in a joint venture, which would force the agencies of justice to operate in a lawful and just manner. It simply means a belief that the prisoner did not use lawful means outside the prison and should therefore be provided more (not fewer) opportunities to learn lawful behavior in the institution. The efforts of the staff should be geared to teaching a prisoner how to use lawful processes to achieve his ends, as well as to accept responsibility for the consequences of his behavior. In the absence of a continuum of justice in the prison, most ends are reached unlawfully. When unlawful behavior in the prison is detected, the standards of due process that we insist upon outside the prison are not applied. The result is a further indication to the convict that lawful behavior for a convict has little payoff. He can be dealt with arbitrarily and usually responds by treating others in the same manner. The justice model would make sure that the prisoner experienced lawful ways of dealing with problems with the expectation that there would be a carry-over to the point of release. The prison experience would try to guarantee that at least for the period of incarceration the prisoner would be exposed to the type of life-style that society expects him to pursue when he is released.

Philosophical Roots

The roots of the justice model theory are deep and seem to be congruent with several disciplines. Cahn, the legal scholar, coined the phrases "the imperial perspective" and "the consumer perspective." [4] Selznick, the sociologist, developed the notion of "private government" and influenced Eliot Studt and Sheldon Messinger's work on the idea of justice as treatment.[5]

Korn and Cressey's ideas of "justice as negotiation" with the demonstration of existing dual systems of justice also contributed to the model. More recently, the philosophic statement by Rawls and the work of Kohlberg and associates have added considerably to giving form to the concept of operational justice as a crucial component of rehabilitation.[6] Disillusionment with the medical model by many behavioral scientists, and the emergence of group and milieu therapy, guided group interaction, self-governance, student revolts, deepening commitments to ideas of participatory democracy and "local control" in the 1960s all helped to influence the development of the model. Selznick has conceptualized the major themes involved in the justice model:

1. *The postulate of normality, competence, and worth.* If offenders are to be dealt with as human beings, it must be assumed that they are basically like everyone else; only their circumstances are special. Every administrative device that negates this principle, and any therapy that ignores it, must be questioned and, if possible, set aside.

2. *Salience of the micro-world.* Men live out their lives in specific settings, and it is there, in the crucible of interaction, that potentialities are sealed off or released. The micro-world is the world of here-and-now; if an inmate's future is to be affected, that future should have a dynamic, existential connection with the experienced present.

3. *The poverty of power.* An administration that relies solely on its own coercive resources can make little contribution to the reconstruction of prison life or to the creation of environments that encourage autonomy and self-respect.

4. *Order as tension and achievement.* Quiescent conformity imposed from above is a parody of social order, not its fulfillment. A system that validates the humanity of its participants, and engages their full resources, accepts the risk of disorder and even, from time to time, of searing confrontations.

5. *Justice as therapy.* A concern for fairness and civic validation should permeate the entire administration of criminal law, including the daily life of the prisoner. That treatment will be most effective which does the most for the inmate's sense of self-worth and responsibility. Nothing contributes more to these feelings than a social environment whose constitutive principle is justice, with its corollaries of participation, giving reasons, and protecting personal dignity.

Without questioning the worth of these objectives, it may be asked: Is it the public policy to punish offenders, especially young offenders, beyond the fact of imprisonment itself? If not, does humane and respectful treatment, not as therapy but as civilized conduct, require a special justification?

In seeking to make criminal justice more redemptive and less punitive, we may have asked too much of institutions that can barely hold their own, let alone develop the competence to be curers of souls. A retreat from rosy hopes may well be inevitable, if only because rehabilitation entails supervision, and ineffective rehabilitation coupled with open-ended control has little to commend it. As the dialogue proceeds and experience is assessed, we may well conclude that the real worth of the "treatment perspective," in its various forms, has been to serve as a civilizing influence on correctional systems. If that should be so, then a theory of corrections that envisions the creation of viable, working communities, based on a postulate of normality, will have most to offer.

It further appears that philosophically the hard deterministic and hard free-will lines have blurred, permitting convicts to be more significant forces in their own lives. There is a softening of the pomposity, even arrogance, that accompanies the role of definer and healer of the behaviorally "sick." The internal struggles of various disciplines, including social work, have produced, if not a more democraticized style, certainly a less authoritarian one.

The field of corrections seems about to move from a conception of offenders as clients to one that views them as constituents. Corrections workers must rid themselves of much (professional) brainwashing. They will have to get on an equal footing with their clientele, and bend every effort—human, financial, and bureaucratic—in their behalf; hence, the conception of "broker" (rather than therapist) for helping a "client" obtain services, and "advocate" (rather than gatekeepers or dispensers) for clients to make sure they get services and just treatment.

Perhaps the simplest way to put it all is that the state cannot, with any degree of confidence, hire anyone to rehabilitate anyone else. This should be evident from past experience. The person troubled or in trouble has to be an equal partner, has to want something to happen. The best way to engage him is to treat him with dignity. Actually, the billions spent on criminal justice are wasted if the offender does not accept the program.

TASKS FOR THE SOCIAL WORK PROFESSION

Will social work have a role in the correctional process of the twenty-first century? Yes, if the profession prepares for it. This entails initially a reassessment of the traditional roles of labelers and processers of deviance. The profession should withdraw, on the practitioner level, from work in prisons. There is nothing of such great specificity in correctional casework that it cannot be performed by contract with existing agencies or private social workers. In corrections, it is of vital importance that the clinician take on an entrepreneurial role. In this way he can remain independent of the correctional agency and assume the role of advocate for his client-constituent. However, the ability to express and act on moral outrage seems to be difficult for professionals who work in correctional agencies. It may be, even less charitably, that for many such employment dulls the ability to develop moral outrage.

Although concern, commitment, and a morality will be essential to social work's new role, they are not enough. It will be necessary to learn and transmit through professional training how administrative agencies make decisions, draw up rules, and distribute power and how to use such knowledge in the service of constituents. Moreover, training should emphasize the client as constituent and service as a joint venture between social worker and client in a quest for justice. For the client-constituent this means that his social worker-advocate will assist him to surmount barriers to service. The expected response by the agencies and the recipient of service is lawful operation and lawful behavior, respectively.

To have a lasting and meaningful impact on corrections the social work profession should develop a set of goals, a strategy for achievement, with a feedback system of evaluation. This is no small task. If corrections suffers fragmentation as a result of federalism, then the profession is even more disabled, with the primary allegiance of its members given to agencies rather than to the profession's standards and its association. Right now the profession is powerless to make an impact on practice in corrections. What meaning would a resolution of NASW's Council on Correctional Services in Social Work, or even of the board of directors, have in relation to a social work department in the Attica Correctional Facility, for example? The irony is that the very progress that individual social workers wish to make is blocked by their inability to perceive themselves as part of a system and to organize their efforts collectively.

Two tasks become necessary: (1) NASW must develop a set of goals and standards for professional practice in corrections, and (2) it must set up enforcement procedures, which in turn means that members must be willing to be guided, judged, and directed by the association rather than by an individual correctional agency's policy. In the last analysis, it reduces to a question of the social worker's confidence in his own competence and power. Corrections is suffering from a vacuum in both leadership and morality, which NASW could help to fill. If it did so, the profession might provide the thrust for institutional change that has been so sorely lacking. Corrections has simply wandered in a maze of small incremental changes fueled by occasional bursts of public outrage and reform that sputter out in public apathy.

Paralleling this process has been a weak professional association subject to traditions and spirited fads. NASW could, through a tough and disciplined effort, provide what has always been missing in corrections— a consistent thrust for institutional change measured aganist an explicated set of goals for professional practice. We are at the threshold of possible dramatic change in corrections. History will record whether NASW was able to intervene and sustain lasting change or whether another watershed in corrections settled into still another century of a dark age.

Finally, social workers need a credibility with their present correctional clientele which they do not enjoy now. The justice model needs thoughtful elaboration, but it represents a dignified reentry point for the profession. A justice model would instantly change a deadening caseload into a willing constituency. It would open the door for a new relationship between professionals and their clientele. If social work wished, it could soon become the conscience of corrections from its present inside vantage point. NASW has members distributed at every level from practitioner to administrator in city, county, state, and federal agencies, in probation, institutional, and parole services. If they would collaborate on a minimal statement of a new purpose based on justice, the twenty-first century could begin a bit sooner.

NOTES AND REFERENCES

1. David F. Greenberg, "Staff Memorandum #2" for the Committee for the Study of Incarceration; and Roger Hood and Richard Sparks, Key Issues in Criminology (New York: McGraw-Hill Book Co., 1970).

2. Hood and Sparks, op. cit., pp. 188–192.

3. Greenberg, op. cit., p. 68.

4. Edmond Cahn, "Law in the Consumer Perspective," University of Pennsylvania Law Review, 112 (1963), pp. 1–210.

5. Eliot Studt and Sheldon Messinger, C-Unit-Men in Quest of a Community in Prison (New York: Russell Sage Foundation, 1971).

6. John Rawls, A Theory of Justice (Cambridge: Harvard University Press, 1972); L. Kohlberg, P. Schars, and J. Hickey, "The Justice Structure of the Prison— a Theory and an Intervention," Prison Journal (Pa.), 51, No. 2 (1971), pp. 3–14.

4

Developing Values Through Milieu Therapy

Essey
Wolfrom

PRISON REFORM proposals, which run the gamut from elimination of prisons entirely to major reforms in established, large prisons, are a popular concern of the day. Some of this concern is based not only upon humanitarian ideals but on cold, hard facts that show that prisons and the sentencing of felons to prisons are deterrents neither to crime nor to a return to crime once the person has left prison. Much support is being given to developing community-based treatment programs for persons convicted of felonies; the aim is to eliminate prisons that isolate a person from the society to which he has had difficulty adjusting. Unfortunately, we are not currently at a stage in our country when we can eliminate all prisons at one stroke in favor of community-based settings. Therefoie, we must continue to support treatment-based prison programs and at the same time hasten the advent of community centers and the elimination of today's prisons.

The Purdy Treatment Center for Women, a new prison for women convicted of felonies and sentenced to the only state prison in the state of Washington, has developed a program that is a form of milieu therapy. This program allows the women as much autonomy and even liberty as is deemed possible within the confines of an institutional program. "Individuality" and "responsibility" are key words and key criteria of performance for both residents and staff. The program calls for a close working relationship between residents and staff. This relationship tends to blur the traditionally separated value systems and the usual social distance between staff and residents. Mutual trust and respect become values for residents and staff alike, up to a point. Differences are still apparent, however, particularly when there is interference with the prime value of a resident—freedom.

THE SETTING

The Purdy Treatment Center for Women was opened on February 22, 1971. With some exceptions, almost all the personnel hired by the superintendent had no previous experience in corrections. Thus the philosophy of the program was evident in the very selection of the personnel. That is, traditional prison programs would not be implemented; instead, the emphasis would be on developing new ways of working with incarcerated women.

The facility resembles a small community college. Five residential units, each housing about thirty-two women, are connected by architectural dividers and form a large enclosed rectangle. In the center of the rectangle are three large buildings; one has offices and the medical-dental clinic; a second, the school building and library, also houses the chapel and game room; the third is the kitchen and dining area, which doubles as a multipurpose room. There are no guard towers. Rather than having a separate staff for each function, staff in the residential units have a dual responsibility for both custody and counseling. On the grounds, but away from the main buildings, is an apartment complex comprising ten apartments that can house two women each. These twenty women are classified as "minimum custody" and in addition have been approved for placement in nearby cities in the work or training release program.

Despite the fact that physical brutality has been almost entirely eliminated as punishment in prisons, it has been difficult to eliminate the psychological degradation and deprivation which come from imprisonment. Such a psychological impact is in itself a form of brutality and perhaps even worse than physical punishment; at the very least, it is exceedingly painful. Sociologists have stressed that major hurts include deprivation of liberty, privacy, goods and services, heterosexual relationships, and autonomy.[1]

The Purdy program is attempting to lessen these deprivations as much as possible. Although restricted to the campus, during the day the women are free to move back and forth between school, library, canteen, dining room, residential units, game room, and so on. The state law provides for furloughs, and these are encouraged since they allow the women to maintain ties with their family and friends rather than to develop close ties with fellow residents in the institution. Women at Purdy may wear their own clothes. They have keys to their individual rooms, and there is no restriction on use of their own television or stereo sets, or other personal belongings as long as they take responsibility for their safekeeping.

There is no restriction on the number of letters they can write. Outgoing mail is not censored; incoming mail is opened and the envelopes shaken to eliminate any contraband, but the mail is not read. There is no restriction on the number of packages the family and friends can send or bring into the institution, although a staff member is present when the residents open the packages. On occasion family and friends may bring in fresh meat, vegetables, or canned goods since the women may cook in their residential units if they wish. There is a telephone in each residential unit and residents are free to use it as long as they maintain common courtesy and do not monopolize it.

Visiting is on both Saturdays and Sundays, and family members may visit in the residential units. In addition, children of women living in the apartments may stay overnight or for weekends. This has done much to alleviate a major deprivation for women which involves the separation and loss of relationship with children.[2]

Although the institution does not provide for conjugal visiting, the staff does support strongly the use of furloughs for maintaining family relations. In addition, about one third of the counseling staff members assigned to the residential units are men. The male counselors give many of the women who have not had an opportunity for a positive nonsexual relationship with a man an opportunity to form such ties. The men are not there, it should be stressed, for security purposes, but as part of a planned counseling service base.

THE PROGRAM

Development of individual programming for each resident is the most important part of the program. This can do much to lessen the adverse psychological impact of the women's loss of autonomy. Unfortunately, at some institutions individual programs have been formulated solely by a staff member or staff committee; residents have not been included in making these decisions.

At Purdy every effort is made to involve the woman in making whatever decisions about herself she is able to. With the exception of the first month of confinement when the women are asked to work in the kitchen facility, there are no assigned work stations or mandatory school participation. When there is an opening to help the staff in the business office, clinic, school office, recreation, or other place, a resident may apply for the job and is interviewed just as she could be in the free world. Counseling staff is available to help her choose the areas that interest her. With the emphasis on individuality and responsibility, a woman may stay up all night since there are no lights-out or lock-up times. If she maintains her commitments to the program, her late hours will create no problem for her. If she does not, this will be discussed and handled with her at an individual planning meeting. At such a meeting a woman may request approval for work and/or training release, early parole, furlough, or a similar change in her program.

Planning meetings for each resident are held about every six to eight weeks; both the staff of the residential unit and the inmate participate. During the meeting the resident discusses with the staff the positive and negative aspects of her program and what her goals are. The staff also tell her their impressions of her progress. Also her participation in school or work may be evaluated with her in terms of her future requests.

Through a special law and justice grant, the regular Purdy staff is augmented by specialists who handle the large work and training release program for the center. About 70 percent of the residents who have been paroled from the institution have participated in this program; 15–20 percent of the total population have been on work or training release at any one time.[3] The work and training release program bases its programming on the decisions and interests of the individual woman. It is implemented in neighboring communities. Women on work release who live in the apartments on the grounds earn standard wages, pay rent to the institution, buy their own food and clothing, and pay for private medical and dental care, which allows them to be at least partially responsible for themselves. Women on training release do not pay for these maintenance items; they are eligible, however, for a daily incentive allowance for spending money.

IMPACT ON STAFF AND RESIDENTS

Traditional prison programs are quite clear-cut. Social distance is emphasized to separate the staff from the residents. Signs of this distance can be seen in the uniforms and nameplates worn by staff and by separate dining facilities. These allow staff members to continue rationalizing reasons for punishment, confinement, and the difference between a "con" and a "cop."

Working so closely with the residents in a program such as that at Purdy tends to break down this traditional distance. It involves a great deal of commitment on the part of staff in the attempt to help motivate a resident and to develop individualized programs. Through this relationship the staff person finds himself realizing that the resident is a person of worth and is likeable. The age range for staff and residents at Purdy is similar, and this also tends to bridge the gap between the staff and residents. A community of interests is apparent in informal and formal "rap" sessions with individuals and groups of staff and residents. The residents and staff begin to trust each other.

In an anonymous questionnaire completed voluntarily by parolees from Purdy, a number of women commented on this point. They noted as beneficial the trust placed in them. They also indicated that they talked more to the staff about their problems and less to fellow residents than might have been expected in traditional settings.[4] As a young resident recently explained:

> Staff and residents have a trustworthy type of commitment to each other in this program. Staff does tend to get involved deeply with residents; usually a counselor will believe in and get to know a resident quite well.
>
> It is hard to relate with staff, because let's face it, we do live in two different worlds, but since I am a first-timer, a convict, and 20 years old, I have somewhat of a yearning to reach out and understand what is going on with people—all people. Maybe that's why I really do see a beginning of changes within this program here at Purdy.

Much of what is being done at Purdy is good and can be a healthy beginning of a new working relationship, but it can be abused. It is easy, particularly for young, new staff members, to become overinvolved in a woman's problems to the detriment of the resident herself. Residents can also use the involvement of the staff for their own purposes.

Again quoting the young resident:

> As the long-time convicts say, "There is game playing." Now I despise playing games, but because the system is so complex and there are so many turns to go the right way, I find it completely necessary to play a game sometimes. After all freedom is my first must, on my list of values.

Every effort must be made to keep the commitment and involvement with the resident on a helping level rather than letting them deteriorate to a level that places the resident in a difficult spot with her fellow residents and even with other staff members. The convict code must be recognized. As the resident says: "The convict code shall always remain, at least until prisons or any resemblance of the prison are destroyed and vanish as part of a need for our society."

CONCLUSION

Not all prison reformers, nor all residents, nor all former residents, can support the foregoing ideas. Persons with differing views include those who would do away with prisons entirely. These advocates maintain that programs such as those described do not reform—they just disguise the factors of degradation by giving them new names.[5]

It is recognized that treatment-based prison programs are new, and this program can only be suggestive, not definitive. Time and continuing research are needed to validate the propositions. However, it seems obvious that the Purdy program has markedly affected the values of the staff. There is evidence that it has an impact on the values of residents. Both staff and residents can support a working relationship based on trust and respect. However, their primary goals are different, and this may separate them. That is, the primary goal of the resident is freedom and that of the staff is rehabilitation.

As good as reform programs in prisons may sound, and, well-motivated as staff may be, the final result must be the impact on the prisoner herself. The program in operation at the Purdy Treatment Center for Women is undoubtedly one of the best. Surely it has application for any prison, whether for men or women.

NOTES AND REFERENCES

1. Rose Giallombardo, *Society of Women: A Study of Women's Prison* (New York: John Wiley & Sons, 1966), chap. 7.

2. David A. Ward and Gene G. Kassebaum, *Women's Prison: Sex and Social Structure* (Chicago: Aldine Publishing Co., 1965), pp. 14–15.

3. "Report of Work and Training Release Program, Purdy Treatment Center for Women, 1971 to 1972." Unpublished report, July 1972; Xeroxed. Available on request to the institution.

4. Gregory L. Goodrich, "Report of the Survey on Parolees." Unpublished manuscript, August 1972; Xeroxed. Available on request to the institution.

5. American Friends Service Committee, *Struggle for Justice: A Report on Crime and Punishment in America* (New York: Hill & Wang, 1971).

5

Child Care for Mothers in Prison

Dorene A. Buckles,

Mary Ann LaFazia

APPROXIMATELY 70 percent of the women incarcerated on felony charges at the Work and Training Release Project at the Purdy Treatment Center for Women in Gig Harbor, Washington have children.[1] From the standpoint of state budgeters and public assistance administrators, the cost of foster care, Aid to Families with Dependent Children grants, day care, and homemaking services plus caseworker salaries is considerable.[2] If the mother does not resume care of the children soon after her release, the costs of long-term care are even greater.

Parolees in a small-scale exploratory research project indicated that from the standpoint of the incarcerated mother, incarceration did have a detrimental effect on their relationship with their children.[3] Moreover, incarcerated mothers with children in foster care indicated in group meetings and individual interviews that in practice, foster care has a detrimental effect on the mother-child relationship over and above the incarceration itself.

From the standpoint of the institution's treatment staff, a woman worried over or defending her role and rights as a mother has little time or energy left to participate in the counseling or rehabilitation resources available to her. Alleged or real injustices or hurts regarding their children are extremely effective red herrings that women can use to avoid personal issues.

From the standpoint of the child welfare service worker, a child who does not understand why he has to be in foster care, or feels he has been deserted by Mom and wonders why, cannot respond to the care and resources offered by foster parents and caseworker.

CONCEPTUAL FRAMEWORK

In recognition of the special problems of incarcerated mothers, a program was set up in 1971 at Purdy Treatment Center in Gig Harbor, Washington. The conceptual framework was as follows:

1. Maternal child care is a responsibility, not a privilege. Regardless of the circumstances of the natural mother, she still has something to offer her child or children, and she is expected to give it. When the mother is absolutely convinced that she is either unable or unwilling to provide adequate care for the children, her relinquishment of her natural rights for the purpose of adoption is one way of fulfilling that responsibility. The foster care program was designed primarily to assist the woman who is willing to assume her responsibilities for her children.

2. Merely because incarceration makes it impossible for the natural mother to assume full responsibility for her child, she should not be deprived of realistic responsibility. Women at Purdy Treatment Center have strongly objected to child welfare workers making decisions regarding a child's life, such as locating a foster home and how frequent visits should be; developing future plans for the child; and the manner in which specific problems are resolved. When the natural mother is involved in such planning, it helps both mother and child when she resumes care. It also alleviates the anxiety described in another study when the mother hears that a decision has been made, but does not know the reasoning behind it.[4]

3. In this particular setting, the child welfare worker serves and treats the child, and the institutional counselor serves and treats the mother. Conflict is minimized by frequent communication and the mutual goal of reuniting the family.

4. In this society, a major part of a woman's identity is tied up with her role as mother, wife, and/or lover. A rehabilitation program concentrating on work or study skills without recognition of this major role treats only parts of the woman.

5. Children need to know where their mother is and why. The fact that she is in prison for a definite reason and will be released at a speci-

fied time is easier for a child to handle than the unknown. The child does not need to fantasize about where his mother is. He can understand the separation as simply a separation rather than a rejection.

THE PROGRAM

In 1972 the Purdy program was staffed by one institutional social worker and one public assistance child welfare worker, both of whom also had a variety of other duties. It served fifteen women from seven counties who had a total of forty-three children. Since it served only women who were referred by other counseling staff, the figures do not represent all women with children at the center. The children served ranged from newborn infants to age 13. Fifty percent of the women were sentenced for grand larceny; other offenses included murder, drugs, prostitution, assault, and armed robbery. Although there are long-term sentences, the average stay at the center ranges from sixteen to eighteen months. Four women have been paroled, and they now have their children with them.

Visits Inside the Center

Plans to strengthen and maintain family ties were built into the center's total program. At the time the center opened, an agreement was reached with the Department of Social and Health Services, the umbrella agency of which both the Division of Institutions and the Division of Public Assistance are parts, that children of women sentenced to the center could be moved to foster homes in neighboring counties to allow for more frequent visits. In addition, it was agreed that when court deprivation hearings were warranted, they should be held as soon as possible so that both mother and child could begin the process of readjustment. However, when there was not sufficient cause for deprivation, the goal should be the reuniting of the family.

The women's children are allowed to visit at any time. Visits take place within the living units. This allows for conversing quietly or taking naps in the mother's private room or socializing with friends and taking part in activities in the living-recreation area. The staff has noted that the residents make a point of tempering their language and behavior while children are present. There is usually no time limit for the length of visits. During extended visits, children eat in the dining room, which serves all residents and staff alike. Women who can afford to pay for their children's meals are expected to do so.

Although the visiting program is reasonably successful, some problems continue to be apparent. The greatest problem is that mothers and children are frequently surrounded by so many friends and well-wishers that there is little time for personal visits. The social worker was besieged with mothers who were concerned about when their child's next visit would take place, and what could be done about foster parents who alienated their children from them or a caseworker who ignored them. In response to these problems, the social worker met with the child welfare worker from a neighboring county, and the two developed a more complete program for mothers with children in foster care.

Foster Care Program in the Center

A resident who wishes to have her child moved closer to the institution consults with her counselor, who may refer the request to the center social worker. The social worker then confers with the child welfare worker who visits the natural mother. Together they discuss the practicality of moving the children. If the mother has only two more months to serve, for instance, the move might be detrimental. This also gives the caseworker an opportunity to learn from the natural mother what type of foster home she would feel comfortable having her children placed in; for example, whether it could be a single-parent home, the preferred number and ages of other children in the home, and the religion of the foster parents. The child welfare worker establishes ground rules with each mother concerning the frequency and length of visits, the feasibility of visiting the foster home, the goal in relation to the time when she would want the children returned to her care. For example, if a woman's minimum sentence is five years and her child is 13 years old, the mother needs to be realistic about the kind of relationship she wishes to establish with her child: whether she should plan with her child toward the day they can live together or help the child face the fact that this foster placement will probably be permanent.

The second step in the program is to find foster parents who can accept the natural mother as a person and not think of her only as a convict. Foster parents are requested to commit themselves to caring for the child for as long as the natural mother is institutionalized. Thus, contrary to traditional foster placements, the length of placement and the natural parents' whereabouts are known, and foster parents can decide whether they are able to work under these conditions.

The foster parents must also agree to transport the children to the institution for visits and to have the natural mother visit their home. They must be willing to share the daily routine of the foster child with the natural mother and include her in any major decision-making, which would also include matters in regard to vacations, dancing lessons, and so on. When a child is presented to the foster parent, the child welfare worker shares with the foster parent all the information available on the child and a little pertinent background on the natural mother. Moreover, the natural mother is given an opportunity to share with the foster parent those aspects of her life she feels comfortable about sharing.

The third step is visits by foster parents, usually the foster mother, to the natural mother at the center. These visits have turned out to be most beneficial, since both foster mother and natural mother can then assess whether they can work with each other. In one incident, the natural mother decided against a particular foster mother, and in another, a foster parent decided against making a commitment to the natural mother and her children. Such contacts have alleviated the necessity of moving a child from one foster home to another.

These visits also allow the foster mother and the natural mother to discuss their mutual expectations and concern for the child and to work out basic items, such as what the natural mother wishes her children to call the foster parent. It becomes the start of a partnership between foster mother and natural mother and is encouraged so that the child is not put into a position of having to choose between them. It is also designed to discourage older children from attempting to pit one against the other. For the toddler who is still trying to learn who he is in relation to his mother, the program is attempting to provide at least consistency in the way his two caretakers treat him and what they expect of him.

After the foster parents have been chosen, the agency that has the child in placement is responsible for preparing the child for the move. Our observation has been that the move is a positive experience for the child because he knows he is nearer his mother. With small children, a visit is made to the mother at the center prior to the move to the new foster home to help the youngster understand that he is near her. The move is also strong evidence to both child and natural mother that the powers that be are really serious in their desire to see the family reunited.

The children visit their mother on a scheduled basis. This allows the child and his natural mother to anticipate each visit and make whatever preparations are necessary. The visits have been quite positive for the children. They are happy and excited to visit their mother, but are ready to return to the foster home and their daily tasks. The natural mother becomes an integral part of the child's life without dominating it, and vice versa.

In the work release program, the mother and another resident share one of ten modern, two-bedroom apartments which have full kitchens. The apartments are located on a hill overlooking the center. A mother can have her children spend a weekend or even longer with her in her apartment, provided she will be home to care for them. This, in addition to regular visits and use of the furlough and special escort programs, enables a woman to spend significant amounts of time with her children.

Natural Mother's Visit to Foster Home

Another aspect of the program is the natural mother's visits to her child in the foster home, to which she is escorted by her institutional counselor. These visits give the natural mother an opportunity to see her child on his grounds. She is also able to relate to the child more realistically than in the "grandmother or visiting aunt" syndrome of gifts and brief exemplary behavior. In the foster home, the natural mother can feed the child lunch; play with him with his toys; see his bedroom, his pets, his hobbies; and so forth. Visiting in the foster home also allows the natural mother to observe family styles different from her own, and the foster mother may become a role model for some natural mothers.

MANAGEMENT OF CONFLICT

The foster mothers and natural mothers also take part in periodic group sessions with the child welfare worker and the social worker. These have been excellent times for negotiation of difficult areas of conflict of interests, such as the natural mother's desire to see the children weekly versus the foster mother's concern about her own energy and the need of the foster family to engage in their own activities. Both sides have been able to hear and respond to the other and to formulate solutions agreeable to all.

When conflict or disagreement occurs with either the foster parents or the natural mother, such as the foster mother not keeping scheduled appointments, or the natural mother not properly feeding the child, the child welfare worker and the center social worker arrange to have them meet and work out their differences with the two staff members included in the meeting. This aspect has alleviated the middleman and troubleshooter role that staff can easily fall into. It also minimizes manipulation of staff by either party.

PROTECTION OF MATERNAL RIGHTS

An important auxiliary service of this program is the ability of residents and center staff to consult with a legal assistance representative. When the resident's legal problems involve children, the legal assistance representative and social worker frequently work together. Usually, problems can be resolved by negotiation with the natural father, relatives, or caseworker. For example, a policy of a child welfare office was altered as a result of a conference between its representatives, the presiding juvenile court judge, the legal assistance representative, the social worker, and a representative from Catholic Children's Services. Newborn babies and children not already temporary wards of the court prior to their mother's incarceration can now be placed in foster care without court wardship.

When negotiation fails, legal representation is made available to the mother whether she is a plaintiff or defendant. Visiting and custody have been the two major areas in which problems have arisen. Legal assistance continues to be a resource to most mothers after they are paroled.

CONCLUSION

After two years of experience with this program, it has been found that natural mothers no longer besiege the social worker with child-related problems, children adjust to foster homes, and foster parents are enthusiastic about having a relationship with the natural mother as well as with the child. After being a part of this program, all four women who were paroled have resumed full care of and responsibility for their children.

There are numerous areas in which similar programs could be tried. For example, the program could be used for foster care of children whose mothers are not incarcerated. In fact, the child welfare worker in this program uses the approach with other foster care cases as well. The program could also be attempted in juvenile institutions with the goal of paroling the child in the care of his family rather than sending him to foster care or group homes. The additional element of family counseling might aid a program in that setting. Incarcerated fathers could also benefit from a similar program. This program already includes one incarcerated father as well as the incarcerated mother. There are exciting possibilities of using a similar program in cases where, although the parent's sentence is less lengthy, the child still tends to get caught in indefinite foster home placements.

Additional research will be needed, but results seem to support the following conclusions:

1.   Foster parents can cope with even a manipulative, demanding "convict"-mother.

2.   Foster parents can relate to the incarcerated natural mother as a person.

3.   Foster parents can enjoy being true substitute parents.

4.   The children of incarcerated mothers can feel, often for the first time in their lives, that all parties concerned—natural mother, foster parents, child welfare worker—are working toward common goals.

5.   The incarcerated woman, given the opportunity to reestablish her role as mother and actually involve herself in parenting, will do so.

6.   Professionally trained and experienced child welfare workers should be included on the staff of women's prisons.

NOTES AND REFERENCES

1.   The annual report (1972) of the Work and Training Release Project at the Purdy Treatment Center for Women indicates that 71 percent of the women have children. Ward and Kasselbaum, *Women's Prison* (Chicago: Aldine Publishing Co., 1965), indicates that 68 percent of the women at the California Institute for Women, Frontera, Calif., had children at the time that book was written.

2.   Actual figures for numbers of children in foster care or on AFDC as a direct result of the mother's incarceration and of fathers and of relatives who use day care and homemaking services as a direct result of the mother's incarceration are not known.

3.   Gregory L. Goodrich, unpublished research project, 1972. Copies of report available through Purdy Treatment Center, Gig Harbor, Washington.

4.   Dorothy Zietz, "Child Welfare Services in a Woman's Correctional Institution," *Child Welfare*, 42 (April 1963), pp. 185–190.

6

Group Relations in Criminal Justice

Ronald I. Weiner

IN THE LAST few years the professional literature has delved more deeply into the problems of police-community relations.[1] Recently, special attention has been focused on the plight of offenders, perhaps as a result of the moral bankruptcy demonstrated by the criminal justice system at the Attica (New York) State Prison in 1971. However, with all that has been stated about the nature of problems inherent in law enforcement, corrections, and social change, little has been written about new training or learning opportunities designed to develop in criminal justice personnel the necessary skills and responsibility for performing their complex tasks.

In 1970 a pilot group relations program was initiated at the American University. The program was designed for criminal justice personnel, minority group members, staff of other social agencies, and incarcerated offenders. The major premise behind this program is that individuals who interact with one another under situations that frequently result in conflict offer each other potential learning opportunities that can be useful in ameliorating tension and reducing conflict. The model for the program was patterned after the work of Rice.[2] The theoretical formulations about groups are those of Bion.[3]

The Library
Saint Francis College
Fort Wayne, Indiana 46808

PROGRAM DESIGN

A basic assumption of the program was that although society exercises authority over individuals and groups in many ways, its most severe and far-reaching sanctions are exercised through its institutions for the administration of civil and criminal justice. Consequently, it is important for personnel in these institutions to understand as fully as possible the impact of their actions on others in the community.

More and more, police and other criminal justice specialists are being confronted by demands that they perform their jobs more responsibly. The recent demands for civil and human rights in prisons [4] parallel similar demands by inner-city residents for humane and responsible behavior by policemen in ghetto areas. Bittner suggests that a policeman "who works up more feeling that he can safely contain is surely not the one to be trusted with anything more demanding than some simple service routine." He further suggests that "a policeman who appreciates the likely consequences of an approach that will cause resentment and indulges in it nevertheless contributes to what he is paid to prevent." [5] Bittner's remarks demonstrate quite clearly one level of current practice among individuals in law enforcement, corrections, and judicial work who exercise licensed authority over the lives of other human beings without having insight into their own behavior.

The pilot group relations program focuses on these problems. It is only when individuals have an opportunity to examine the manner in which they exercise authority on behalf of their institutions, and test this against reality, that they can reasonably be expected to become more responsible in performing their duty. Consequently, an experimental workshop course, "Problems in the Exercise of Institutional Authority," was created. Students in these workshops were chosen from law enforcement, correctional, probation and parole, judicial, legislative, social service, educational, inner-city, and offender populations. Would-be members were interviewed by experienced social workers and psychologists; those who overtly displayed manifestations of emotional disturbance were advised to postpone their enrollment. The reason given was that the experience might prove to be too stressful for them.

The enrolled students spent the first six days in intensive group relations exercises. The major goals of the program were to provide four types of learning opportunities: (1) to experience and learn to understand something about the nature and exercise of their own authority as a means of helping them to become more responsible in their work and in other social situations; (2) to examine what hinders or facilitates a group in performing a joint task, by focusing on both overt and covert processes as they occur in the context of a variety of group exercises; (3) to learn about the relationship between their own behavior and the behavior of the organizations that they represent through their exercise of authority, as well as maintain task boundaries in terms of space and time; and (4) to explore the problems of leadership in the context of group activity in performing a specific external task.

The educational program to accomplish these objectives consisted of four different types of learning experiences, each designed to represent an abstraction of working life. Rice stresses that "each part of a complex institution has its own distinct primary task which differentiates it from other parts and from the whole, and each contributes to the primary task of the whole." [6] Thus the students were given different opportunities to examine authority relationships, with each exercise designed to have its own primary task.

The Small Study Group

The members of the workshop were divided into five heterogeneous small study groups of twelve or fifteen each and a consultant. The task of each group was to give the members opportunities to study their interpersonal relationships in the here and now, and members were informed that this was *their* task. The consultant's only job was to interpret the group's behavior and his own contribution to it.

The members had no tags to identify themselves or their agencies behind which they could hide, and consequently they had to develop their own means of studying their behavior with the services of the consultant. The consultant provided no formal structure other than by arriving and leaving exactly on time. The consultant's adherence to the task and his neutral position helped the members to focus on his interpretations.

The Large Group

The second major exercise was the large group event, consisting of sixty members and the five consultants. The task of the large group was also to provide learning opportunities but in a larger setting than any one group could form in a face-to-face group. Consequently, the major difficulty was that members not only had to face members from their own study groups but also from other study groups with whom they had no formal contact. Again, since the task of the group was to study its own behavior, the members were free to discuss whatever they pleased. The consultants behaved as they did in their small groups, adhering to the task at all time.

The Intergroup Exercise

The third major learning exercise, and perhaps the one most closely related to police-community relations or inmate-staff relationships, was the intergroup exercise. Here the task was to study the relationships between and among groups as they developed. Members formed their own groups on whatever basis they chose. As a consequence, they could examine the relationships between and among groups as they interacted with each other, involving problems of representation, that is, of exercising authority on behalf of others and of drawing and crossing boundaries. For example, when members spontaneously formed a group, they began to assume an identity with, and a loyalty to, that group, which raised questions about their loyalty to their respective small study groups or personal loyalties to colleagues who were members of the workshop.

There were two distinct and clearly definable groups: the members and the staff. To heighten the learning experience, the consultants formed their own group with their own defined territory in another room. This was somewhat analogous to situations in which police and welfare rights workers might occupy their respective "turf" or, perhaps, when inmates who have gained control of a prison are confronted by armed guards and police. Members could ask the consultants to help them study their relationships between and among groups, including the staff group. Although the members were allowed to do whatever they wished, they were psychologically responsible for whatever authority they exercised individually or collectively on behalf of their respective groups. Groups were forced to develop internal mechanisms to deal with the kind of authority they would allow their members to exercise in their behalf when interacting with the other groups. These processes were open to study by the entire membership.

The Application Group

The fourth major exercise was the application group, which took place during the last two days of the workshop. The task was to consider the relevance of the entire workshop experience to the members' normal work situations. Important in this context was the emphasis not only on what members had learned about the dynamics of their own behavior and that of others, but also on how they were made aware of the dynamics of an institution and its organizational relationships. The understanding of organization dynamics creates an additional and perhaps more important element in the total system of work which emphasizes "justice."

Members were divided into groups that were as homogeneous as possible so far as their jobs were concerned. In this exercise, the learning was related to past work experiences in the light of new knowledge gained during the workshop. A variety of techniques was used such as case conferences, role-playing, and discussions. The workshop ended with the application group because it dealt with the practical problems of the members. Moreover, the members were most concerned at that time with what they were able to take back with them into their own work.

In addition to these primary experiences were the opening plenary session and the closing review session, which marked the systemic basis of this learning model. The opening plenary session served as an introduction to the workshop and presented the staff to the members as a separate group. It also provided an opportunity for the members to raise preliminary questions.

The conference review session allowed the members to discuss the total workshop experience and taught them how to close boundaries. The consultants concentrated on helping the members to understand the dynamics that had occurred during the six days as they raised questions or commented on the workshop experience. The staff did not grade the participants, since it had been pointed out in advance that no attempt would be made to prescribe what anyone should learn and that learning was an individual responsibility.

MAJOR THEMES

During the past two years, six such group relations workshops have been conducted. The dynamics emerging from each workshop differed in their manner of expression. However, the work has revealed at least three common intertwined themes, or dynamics, which reveal significant patterns about the behavior of criminal and civil justice institutions.

Feelings of Inadequacy and Guilt

One major theme was a clear expression on the part of criminal justice workers of inadequacy, guilt, and, to some degree, self-hate in attempting to perform their work without the requisite professional skills, especially the interpersonal skills required for working with others. For example, in several workshops the theme of self-deprecation was expressed loudly on the part of first-line criminal justice personnel who work on the street or in prisons. This dynamic surfaced with the members viewing themselves as "paid leaders" who experience conflict and anxiety in attempting to perform their tasks at a high level of competence. They made comments such as, "We're paid to be leaders" and, "We're all paid to be good counselors and do good therapy without really knowing how."

Somewhat related to this general theme was the notion held by the criminal justice personnel that they had nothing to offer to the learning process. For example, it appeared to the staff that the law enforcement and correctional officers unconsciously colluded with one another to develop a culture that prohibited them from expressing feelings (except perhaps hostility) about themselves and other group members. These personnel frequently stated that "men" did not express such feelings— that they should be "tough." In fact, criminal justice personnel, particularly police officers, saw their situation as analogous to that of "prisoners" who seek to accomplish complex tasks successfully despite limited training. Consequently, they resisted learning in fear that more would then be expected of them by the community than they could possibly give. A dimension of this fear—in fact, almost total denial—emerged in several small study groups when criminal justice personnel avoided any such discussion even though the hostility expressed toward them by offenders and black community members was intense. This dynamic has been pointed out by Bard, who commented: "Fear is a taboo topic among police and [it is] a myth to believe that they do not experience it." He further stated that police agencies seek to prevent their officers from expressing their genuine fears since "there is no formal training provided to police for the exercise of judgment and the use of discretion." [7]

Scapegoating

A second critical dynamic was the scapegoating of offenders and minority group members in the workshops. In one of the early workshops, these scapegoats united and suggested that policemen perpetuate crime in the ghetto through their own illegal activities, such as selling narcotics confiscated in raids, taking bribes for allowing policy games, and receiving payoffs for other favors. Offenders pointed out that they were particularly the victims of police scapegoating because law enforcement officials were covering up for this massive corruption and graft, encouraged by low hiring standards, inadequate compensation, ineptness, and lack of sophistication in controlling organized and white-collar crime. In essence, they felt that the police were organized by the white power structure to concentrate their enforcement efforts on lower-class street crime, and their low hiring standards and salaries fostered a culture that reinforced graft as a definite means of ignoring the issue of the more sophisticated white-collar and organized crime operations. Their accusation was given credence when criminal justice personnel were unable to explain intelligently why there was a disparity in sentencing poor minority group offenders and the "Bobby Bakers" who are occasionally caught and convicted or why consumer protection laws, civil rights laws, housing code violations, and so forth are not adequately enforced. They also cited examples of police officers, probation officers, and particularly correctional officers, who bait offenders into acting out by humiliating references to their manhood, their mothers, and their race, so that the criminal justice worker would then have justification for attacking them physically or having them arrested or locked up for assaulting an officer. There was mild snickering at these accusations but little denial except for the rebuttal that, "Whatever the animals get they deserve."

This dynamic of scapegoating was dramatically acted out in the third workshop during an intergroup exercise when the black community members, offenders, and health and welfare workers indicted the entire criminal justice system by staging a mock trial and accusing the system of perpetuating crime in the ghetto by scapegoating the poor and brutalizing offenders. In a manner that mirrored what they considered typical "justice" in a "white man's court," they barred the criminal justice workers from the room. During the dramatization, the "jury" reached a quick and severe verdict without bothering to take into consideration any of the causes for the system's organizational dysfunction. In much the same way, they perceived that the system did not bother to consider the reasons that most poor offenders commit crimes. Most of the members of the workshop were deeply affected by the demonstrated viciousness they perceived in the system. As a result, the group of approximately fifteen policemen and correctional officers were treated contemptuously by other workshop members. This group found itself in the position of reversing roles with the blacks and offenders in that its members were literally called the "niggers" and "cons" of the workshop. In the process, they began to experience a sense of dehumanization until a point was reached where some of them acknowledged that their plight was much like that of the offender.

During the fourth workshop, in a large group event, scapegoating emerged in a different manner. The police officers had separated themselves from the rest of the workshop participants. Several of them verbally attacked a black representative of a community agency for reading a newspaper and wearing his hat during the session. The black representative walked out and was joined by five other black participants, who returned shortly afterward and seated themselves on either side of the only black consultant in the workshop, opposite the police. They remained in total silence for the remainder of the session, even when negative comments were made about their behavior or when questions were directed to them. This action infuriated the police members, who then began to ask the black females why "the brothers" were silent. One black woman took the bait and asked the group of black men what they hoped to accomplish by their silence. The men did not respond until the last minute of the exercise when one said: "We're not dancing to the tune of the music anymore." The men made it clear that they would not be manipulated by the persons representing the power structure—that they would maintain a sense of identity and pride and deal with the group when and how they chose.

Relationship Between Personnel and Their Employing Institutions

The third dynamic was the relationship between the criminal justice personnel and their respective organizations. For example, the policemen often spoke of wanting only to "put in their time" (usually twenty years) so they could retire on a reasonably substantial pension, regarded as a reward for loyal service. They mentioned the desire to perform a valuable service for the community in a highly competent and professional manner. In fact, some felt they were required to sell their souls, so to speak, to their organizations and believed they were not permitted to question the implications of their actions. This feeling resulted in feelings of resentment toward and mistrust of the institutions, particularly when they were made to see instances of scapegoating.

One group described a situation in which a police inspector who commanded an internal affairs division had been transferred to an obscure assignment simply because one of his subordinates had used poor judgment in accepting a loan from an individual under investigation by the department. Although the inspector had reported to his superiors his own routine investigation of the situation, he was nevertheless transferred several months later when the story was publicized in the newspaper. He subsequently appeared on television, bravely stressing the fact that he was not going to be used and blamed when he had performed his duty by notifying the higher-level command of his findings. The police members in the workshop felt bitter about the incident and cited similar instances. However, they seemed to accept this scapegoating as a normal occupational hazard and realized that even though the inspector had spoken up, no one had come to his defense. In discussing the dynamics of this process, the officers were still reluctant to accept the fact that their own silence and lack of support for their commanding officer had helped reinforce the injustice. The offenders were quick to point out that the very institutions organized to uphold the law and administer "justice" when it suited their convenience often victimized not only powerless minority group members but also the individuals working within the system.

On a somewhat different but related level, offenders and the inner-city community residents continuously castigated representatives from the criminal justice system along with other group members who came from a variety of social service agencies. The predominantly black inner-city and offender groups worked diligently to demonstrate examples of inhumanity heaped on them by each of these agencies. At first the criminal justice and social service workers denied being inhuman, but admitted they could easily understand how their behavior might be so interpreted, given the fact that they attempted to perform their jobs in an "objective" manner without showing any "partiality." The social service workers particularly developed a great sense of guilt over these accusations. They then acknowledged the accusations by statements such as, "Your institution helps to protect you from our humanity." They felt that a variety of policies and procedures were designed to ward off close involvement with the people to be served, whether in a prison, a mental health agency, or a public welfare office.

The members were beginning to work through their feelings of guilt. They recognized that their agencies rewarded them more for efficient reports and statistical records than for helping people. Many workers stated that their agencies were quick to focus on the "negative behavior" of the persons coming to the agencies and that this was an excuse either for not working hard to help them or not working with them at all. Many probation and parole officers admitted that they divided their caseloads into two categories: those they could leave alone entirely because they had minimal problems and those they could forget about because, owing to the little time these workers had to spend with them, they would eventually "break bad" and get into more trouble. These workers spoke cynically and despairingly of not doing much in their jobs; they felt that all they did was "keep the judges happy" by completing pre-sentence reports on cases to which they would devote little time in supervising or in assisting with their problems. They strongly implied that their agencies were not really organized to work with people and that they really did not have the skills necessary for working with offenders.

Some of the police and correctional workers acknowledged feelings similar to those expressed by the probation and parole personnel. For instance, a few policemen suggested that their agencies helped to bring out inhumanity in others by virtue of the people they hired. However, they were unwilling to report specific instances of inhumane conduct on the part of their colleagues and, most often, chose to "look the other way." They rationalized their actions as an occupational necessity, stressing they would risk losing their jobs if they appeared at a hearing brought against one of their colleagues. The consultants pointed out how similar this situation is to the veil of secrecy and the culture of silence of prisoners and to the inmates' code of not "ratting" on their fellow prisoners. It was difficult for the police to accept this comparison. In one workshop they accused the offenders of being "hustlers" who were unwilling to work at normal jobs and instead chose crime as a means to obtain "easy money." The offenders, in turn, answered that "hustling" is hard work; it requires a great deal of ingenuity and creativity and is "handsomely rewarded." They pointed out that legitimate working opportunities were limited, or sometimes unavailable. In addition, they cited a number of examples of what they regarded as pimping and prostitution by criminal justice workers who are enticed to stay in their jobs by pensions, graft, and promotional opportunities. Although the criminal justice workers attempted to deny the accusations or to say they were exaggerated, everyone in the workshop admitted knowing specific instances of this type of behavior in their agencies. What, however, the criminal justice workers found most difficult to accept was the following comment by a high-ranking police official: "We'll have to come to grips with our own inner prostitution before we can really be of help to others and administer 'justice' fairly."

The policemen in the group began to feel that the workshops had put them in touch with themselves to the extent that they could no longer hide behind their ignorance. However, their new awareness posed new problems for them. They felt that if they spoke up, they would face reprisals and would not be able to survive in their jobs. The consultants interpreted this concern as ambivalence toward changing their behavior without any assurance of reward or lack of reprisal.

IMPLICATIONS

By focusing attention almost exclusively on the deviant behavior of offenders and those who seek help from other agencies, social service workers have avoided examining the organizational behavior of these agencies, the behavior of their workers, and how the dynamics and culture within them help to perpetuate the problems they seek to ameliorate.

Accountability

Wolfgang suggests that the criminal justice system is a failure because "it has no moral conscience, no need to report to its immediate neighbors, let alone external agents. Thus it has become an index of our decadence, of our failure to treat each man as a part of humanity, of the pressure of numbers upon a bureaucracy that becomes bereft of emotions." [8] He further stresses the need for those who work in the criminal justice system to be accountable for their actions—a need that should apply equally to all public agencies which exercise legitimate authority over other human beings. We have a professional and an ethical responsibility to counter his assumption that "there is inadequate display of what in fact goes on in the police department, in the district attorney's office, and in the operation of the courts, probation, parole and prisons." [9] Moreover, without establishing a mechanism for examining the operations and behavior of social and criminal justice institutions, society justifies the kind of moral bankruptcy that often results in an Attica State Prison riot or in a mass arrest of those who attend a political demonstration.

A mechanism must be developed to break down the veil of secrecy in criminal justice and public service agencies and to open them up to careful public scrutiny. Wilson believes, for example, that most police departments are committed to a strategy of secrecy, which is "one of the most important ways by which policemen defend themselves against the presumed hosility of civilians." [10] This, perhaps, is also true of other criminal justice agencies, particularly prisons and probation and parole departments.[11] One method of developing a means of ensuring accountability in the system might be to establish local criminal justice councils that are independent of public governmental control. Various professional and civic associations and representatives from the university community and from various community groups that utilize legal and other community organization strategies could form a coalition to work to develop standards of accountability. Local chapters of NASW could assume leadership in creating such a coalition as part of their commitment to advocacy.

Decision-Making by Offenders

Offenders must be given opportunities to participate actively in making decisions about programs that directly affect their lives. The totally dehumanizing model of decision-making that does not allow offenders any such responsibility can no longer be tolerated. For example, offenders might help develop specific criteria for recommending probation or granting parole, rules regulating probation or parole supervision, and rules and penalties for violating prison codes. Their input might encourage them to react more responsibly to procedures they believe to be reasonable and fair.

Segal thinks that, in many respects, the social regulatory model, which focuses attention on changing the behavior of the "deviant" individual, is invalid. He supports the idea that change in the criminal justice system can only come about when "the politicalization of deviance, particularly in institutions, through consumer participation will make the conflict visible, and inmates will undoubtedly demand changes in institutional hierarchies." [12] Segal further suggests that "social workers must understand that the thrust toward politicalization of deviance is in part to counteract the abuses perpetrated on the deviant in the name of therapy and rehabilitation." [13]

Education

Educational institutions offering courses in the criminal justice system have an opportunity and a responsibility to link their curricula with what the students will actually find when they work in the system. Also their curricula should help the student find means of increasing and improving his performance of tasks in a way that will be beneficial to society in general. The writer's own experience with the pilot group relations program demonstrates the value of criminal justice workers and minority group members working together and learning from one another. Although it has been painful for some, students recognize some of their deficiencies; at the same time, they want to improve their performance so they may find greater satisfaction in their jobs and reduce the risk of being injured. Bard, from his own work with the police, comments on this point:

> It is our impression also that policemen themselves feel more secure and less defensive generally when they have professional skills equal to the increasing complexities of their role. To lessen the gap between community and the police, law enforcement personnel can generate respect and trust by performing their complex order-maintenance functions in ways that are consistent with the citizens' hopes.[14]

A critical learning objective for future work with criminal justice students is to help them focus on the demands their organizations and the larger society have on them and the effects on their outlook and performance. It would seem important to allow students opportunities to learn about the behavior and culture in their own institutions so they will know what they must sacrifice of themselves in order to live within them. Rice's comments on this process should be carefully appraised:

> All managers, administrators, and professional workers, in whatever field the work, have to use more than techniques; at a minimum they have to come to terms with themselves, and with the personal and group characteristics of those who man the institutions in which they work. To be successful they have to make constructive use of their own personalities.[15]

Criminal justice workers must also be given opportunities to examine the manner in which society uses them to combat basic social and racial injustice. Marx helps to clarify this point: "It is increasingly clear that police are unduly scapegoated, stereotyped, and maligned; they are, as well, underpaid, undertrained, given contradictory tasks, and made to face directly the ugly consequences of the larger society's failure to change." [16]

Education for criminal justice workers must begin to focus on the body of knowledge required for performing complex tasks. For example, they must have opportunities to conceptualize and experience the meaning of behavior expressed by individuals from different sociocultural backgrounds. This does not mean merely giving them a course in race relations. These are men of action who desire a sense of excitement and challenge that requires a learning model which will allow them to participate actively in the learning process. The laboratory model, group dynamics, psychodramatic techniques, group relations workshops, and similar approaches provide the means for achieving learning in experiential ways which offer hope for reducing conflict.

One might begin to think of these educational efforts with criminal justice workers and minority group members as being change-agent oriented. Can social workers, for example, begin to develop educational models that stress the responsibility and authority that students exercise on behalf of their institutions while recognizing that their behavior must demonstrate trust and accountability? This will require a commitment to them that they are capable of changing their behavior in ways the community will regard as responsible and professional. If social workers, as educators, can help them in learning to experience and acquire new skills, help them to see their potential value as change agents and preventive agents rather than as mere law enforcers, their progress toward professionalization will be enhanced and society will be assisted to expect competence from them in dealing with crime in an intelligent manner. In essence, sights must be set on helping them develop their potential for becoming the "informed, deliberating, and technically efficient professional who knows that he must operate within the limits set by a moral and legal trust." [17]

NOTES AND REFERENCES

1. Egon Bittner, *The Functions of the Police in Modern Society*, Public Health Service Publications No. 2059 (Washington, D.C.: U.S. Government Printing Office, 1970), p. 121; John J. Hughes, "Training Police Recruits for Service in the Urban Ghetto—a Social Worker's Approach," *Crime and Delinquency*, 13 (April 1972), pp. 176–184; Kenn Rogers, "Group Processes in Police-Community Relations," *Bulletin of the Menninger Clinic*, September 1972, pp. 515–532.

2. A. K. Rice, *Learning for Leadership* (London: Tavistock Publications, 1965).

3. Wilfred Bion, *Experience in Groups* (New York: Basic Books, 1959).

4. *See* Samuel Melville, *Letters from Attica* (New York: William Morrow & Co., 1972).

5. Bittner, op cit., p. 121.

6. Rice, op. cit., p. 18.

7. Morton R. Bard, "New Strategies of Law Enforcement." Paper presented at the University of Maryland Institute for Criminology, May 13, 1971.

8. Marvin E. Wolfgang, "Making the Criminal Justice System Accountable," *Crime and Delinquency*, 18 (January 1972), p. 15.

9. Ibid., p. 16.

10. James Q. Wilson, "The Police and Their Problems: A Theory," in Arthur Niederhoffer and Abraham S. Blumberg, eds., *The Ambivalent Force: Perspectives on the Police* (Waltham, Mass.: Ginn & Co., 1970), p. 303.

11. Tom Murton and Joe Hyanes, *Accomplices to the Crime: The Arkansas Prison Scandal* (New York: Grove Press, 1969).

12. Brian Segal, "The Politicalization of Deviance," *Social Work*, 17 (July 1972), p. 46.

13. Ibid.

14. Morton R. Bard, *Training Police as Specialists in Family Crisis Intervention* (Washington, D.C.: U.S. Government Printing Office, 1970), p. 29.

15. Rice, op. cit., p. 7.

16. Barry T. Marx, "Civil Disorder and the Agents of Social Control," *Journal of Social Issues*, 26 (1970), p. 55.

17. Bittner, op. cit., p. 121.

7

The Prisoners' Rights Movement

Louis Schneiderman

THE CIVIL RIGHTS ACT of 1964 permits civil action by any person, including a prisoner, against prison administration and/or its personnel, for "deprivation of any rights, privileges or immunities secured by the Constitution and laws." [1] The growing number of suits won in the courts and the monetary penalties imposed on prison administrators suggest that the rights of prisoners are being taken seriously. Indeed, sheriffs and jailers are cautioned in a manual for jail administrators that they may be held personally liable for failure to provide a prisoner "his right to safe custody and humane treatment." This caution adds: "He [the prisoner] may recover for negligent and intentional injuries, regardless of who inflicts them." [2] And "A Model Act for the Protection of Rights of Prisoners" states that "a new element has been added to prisoner grievances: an assertion both of positive rights and of the right to be protected against abuse." [3]

TYPES OF RIGHTS

What are prisoners' rights? Do these rights change? In what direction? Primarily, prisoners' rights have been identified and have evolved out of the progressive changes in court interpretations of the U.S. Constitution and its amendments. The growing weight of concerned opinion for the wider spread of democratic principles and individual rights and for more therapeutically effective correctional systems to protect society against the mounting volume of crime contributes to such judicial considerations. These rights are as follows.

Religious Observance

Recognizing that freedom of religion is protected under the First Amendment, prisoners have brought suit for extension of that right to them while in prison. Black Muslim prisoners have been responsible for many recent petitions that led to judicial rulings in support of this right for them. However, the U.S. Supreme Court limited the right and distinguished between two concepts embodying the First Amendment, namely, "the freedom to believe and the freedom to exercise one's belief . . . the first is absolute and the second is not, and furthermore, the freedom to act is subject to regulation for the protection of Society. This latter concept is clearly applicable to a penal institution." [4] The freedom of Black Muslims in prison to hold their religious beliefs was recognized, but the freedom to exercise such beliefs was limited, and subject to prison regulation to avoid riots and any other serious breach of prison discipline.

Mail

Rights of prisoners to send mail to, and receive it from, any source without prison censorship also became subject to judicial review under the First Amendment. Courts rejected censorship of mail except for some limited incoming mail related to issues of security.[5]

Peaceful Assembly

No court case involving prisoners and the First Amendment could be located. One might speculate, nevertheless, on the possibility of the right to peaceful political assembly and, therefore, to organize for furtherance of group interests, inclusive of bargaining potential for better conditions for prisoners, including work, food, medical services, recreation, training, visitors, discipline, and education. The recurrence of riots and other challenges to prison administration currently so often in the news, together with prisoners' demands, suggest some form of de facto negotiations going on between prison administrations and prisoners. Illustrative of this are two news articles which reported that New York State Correction Commissioner Oswald would accept twenty-eight listed proposals by the Attica State Prison rioters and that the warden of the federal correctional institution at Danbury, Connecticut, and the deputy director of the U.S. Bureau of Prisons met with a committee of inmates and asked them to halt their work stoppage pending negotiation of grievances.[6]

Discipline and Punishment

The Eighth Amendment clause against infliction of cruel and unusual punishment was also seen as applicable to prisoners' rights. Judge Blackmun gave the following written opinion in 1966:

> We have a flat recognition that the limits of the 8th Amendment prescription are not easily or exactly defined, and we also have a clear indication that the applicable standards are flexible, that disproportion both among punishment and between punishment and crime, is a factor to be considered, and that broad and idealistic concepts of dignity, civilized standards, humanity and decency are useful and usable.[7]

Judge Spaeth extended this concept further, emphasizing overpowering cumulative effects, and stating in part that forcing a prisoner to eat only with a spoon, serving coffee with cream and sugar in it, using summary disciplinary proceedings, allowing a prisoner to earn money only by subjecting his body to medical experimentation, administering the "cold-turkey" treatment to addicts, wasting inmates' time by enforced idleness, allowing contact with visiting family members only by means of a tube in a partition, are measures that exceed the limits of standards of decency.[8]

Two separate petitions by prisoners submitted in two different courts protesting that confinement in the given prisons was cruel and unusual punishment are also of major significance. In one case, the Federal District Court held that, "As as the Court is aware, this is the first time that convicts have attacked an entire penitentiary system. The Court sustains the claim that conditions and practices in the Penitentiary System are such that confinement of persons therein amounts to cruel and inhuman punishment prohibited by the 8th and 14th Amendments." The court retained jurisdiction and gave the Arkansas authorities time to eliminate abuses.[9] In the other case, the Philadelphia Court of Common Pleas condemned the city's Holmesburg Prison because conditions in the prison constituted cruel and inhuman punishment, ordered the transfer of the two petitioners, and retained jurisdiction to ensure that the prison administration eliminated the abuses.[10]

Legal Help

This category covers many areas of prisoners' concern with their rights and is associated with the due process clause of the Fourteenth Amendment. In 1966 the Fourth Circuit Court stated that "imprisonment does not remove a prisoner's right to be free from arbitrary sanction." [11] The decision made by U.S. District Court Judge J. Robert Mehrige enjoined prison officials from punishing prisoners for their attempt to obtain legal help.[12] In another situation, the court affirmed the right of "jailhouse lawyers" to aid other prisoners, thus reinforcing the rights of prisoners to have access to legal materials and to petition government for redress of grievances.[13] The weight of responsibility in the due process issue in relation to prison administration involving disciplinary hearings and decisions was stated by the court:

> This Court recognized that there are legitimate administrative considerations that cannot be ignored in devising a disciplinary procedure that complies with constitutional standards of due process; and it has no intention of imposing on prison administration a disciplinary procedure impractical of implementation. . . . However, the fundamental nature of the rights involved persuades the Court that a heavy burden rests upon the prison officials to insure that the disciplinary procedure will be fair.[14]

Issues involving other prison rules, medical care, work, and other such matters, will undoubtedly continue to be brought to court.

COMMUNICATION BETWEEN INMATES AND SOCIETY

In addition to legislative, administrative, and judicial actions that have contributed to clarifying and developing prisoners' rights, there are other factors that have added force to this movement. Prison sentences, other than some life sentences, carry an expectation that prisoners will be prepared to return to free society able to cope with the demands of living without recidivism. This requires a use of the controlled prison environment that permits maximum continuing communication between the inmate and society to facilitate the process of training and learning for such resocialization. Implicit is the basic philosophical shift from the traditional "custody-and-security" emphasis to resocialization. Also implicit is the development of channels of communication between administration and staff on the one hand, and inmates on the other, to achieve this shift. Such continuing communication is possible when a base of trust is established in a common objective, such as examining and improving institutional living conditions to permit more fully the meeting of the goal of resocialization. The correctional field is currently in a state of transition and therefore has quite variable administrative emphases as to its direction. Some attempts are being made by different correctional systems to identify communication and other problems of inmates in a restrictive prison society, and their resolution is being attempted, albeit sporadically. For this, some limited elements of community support have already existed. Private community service agencies, such as the John Howard League and correctional service agencies, sometimes with legislative authority, showed not only the outsider's concern for the care and treatment that inmates receive in prison, but also, in effect, identified the prisoner as a continuing and, in time, returning member of society. The self-help movement of various handicapped subgroups of our society added some limited acceptance of both the individual worth of prisoners and their potential for help, currently or later, to others in the same or a similar situation.

INMATE ADVISORY COUNCILS

The expansion of this movement in the correctional field is noted not only in the increasing use and employment of paraprofessional former prisoners as adjuncts of treatment efforts in prisons and related community-based treatment centers, but also in regular staff positions, including that of warden.[15] Furthermore, a growing number of organizations of former prisoners, including for example the Barbed-Wire Society, the Fortune Society, and the Seven Step Foundation, aim at developing public understanding of issues in corrections and engage in efforts with correctional administration, or through legislative or court action, to improve the welfare and rights of prisoners. The thrust of the movement for modifying the institutional milieu to make it more like free society is also derived from the growing professionalization of the correctional field. Such professionalization provides support to correctional administrators convinced of the desirability of such possible shifts. Early attempts in this direction include various short-lived experiments by charismatic correctional administrators in inmate self-government. They ranged from the early establishment of the Mutual Aid League of 1885 in the Jackson (Mich.) Penitentiary to the Norfolk plan in the State Prison Colony in Norfolk (Mass.), established in 1927. Only the latter, however, included both an inmate council and the correctional staff as jointly responsible in the community government.[16] More current efforts at enlisting inmate participation in commerce by government in the penal institutions are more modest, largely in terms of establishing inmate councils on an advisory basis. Discretion and approval for their existence generally seem to rest with the heads of the individual institutions. This might be interpreted as only lukewarm backing by central correctional administrations and therefore as qualified support for increased communication with inmates and for their contributions to their welfare. In the U.S. Bureau of Prisons, "many institutions have sanctioned inmate councils." [17] Inmates advisory councils also exist at the state and local levels.

The preamble to the constitution of the Inmate Advisory Council of the Maine State Prison emphasizes communications and mutual objectives as follows: "In order to create an effective and reliable means of communication between inmates and the administration, and furtherance of mutual objectives intended to foster cooperation and participation in constructive programs, the Inmate Advisory Council is hereby authorized . . ." In October 1971, these inmates attempted to elect "shop stewards" and make "demands," with threat of a strike. The Inmate Advisory Council was suspended for a month. Probably the acting warden saw the council as a feasible but problematic administrative instrument. He mentioned that two correctional officers' unions expressed negative feelings about inmates knowing more of what was going on in the institutions. He therefore also had to give time separately to an elected officers council. He made no reference to the disruption of the informal power balance between inmates and guards resulting from a formal inmate advisory council in direct continuing contact with the warden.

A closer look at the level of development of the prisoners' rights movement suggests some acceptance of inmate advisory councils as a viable tool for prison operation more consonant with current concepts of prison purpose. By and large, prison administrators, if and when they do accept inmate councils, see them as advisory.

The director general of the Swedish National Correctional Administration stated in 1971: "The Administration declared its positive views on the rights of inmates to form advisory councils. . . . There is nothing [in Swedish law] to prevent the inmates of penal institutions from forming their own organizations . . . or for elected bodies within the institutions to further their demands." He further indicated that in October 1970, a hunger strike at Osteraker Central Prison was "supported by a large portion of the country's inmates who went on a sympathy strike," adding that "support was given in various ways by organizations outside the institution." Whether "organizations outside the institution" refers to more than other inmate advisory councils is not clear. He concluded that "the negotiations which started November 30, 1970, at Osteraker

Prison are unique in history. They placed on an equal footing the delegates of the country's 5,000 prisoners on one side and representatives of the correctional authorities and the personnel organizations on the other." [18] Recent correspondence advises that, following an impasse in discussions in November 1971 between inmate representatives and the National Correctional Administration, the inmates met with a top-level committee set up by the Ministry of Justice to consider direction and priorities in the handling of prisoners.[19]

PRISONERS' UNIONS

In the United States, it is noted, there is currently some movement for increasing prisoners' rights and prisoners' participation beyond advisory council status. A 1972 news report states:

> An organization called the United Prisoners Union says it has a cadre of some 3,000 California convicts, former inmates and members of their families . . . and set out to form a national union for the country's 200,000 prison inmates. . . . Inmates and former convicts of prisons in New York, Michigan, Ohio, and Pennsylvania were reported to be responding to the organizing appeals.

It goes on to quote the executive director of the Los Angeles American Civil Liberties Union:

> We are supporting their efforts because of our deep interest in prison reform. . . . Court action may be brought seeking to force prison authorities to admit the union's literature and testing the right of prisoners to organize and of former convicts to hold union office.[20]

The National Labor Relations Act in 1959 (Public Law 86–257) and the related state Public Employees Relations acts may become the vehicles for court action on union organization by prisoners. An attorney of the Community Legal Services in Delaware recently advised that a majority of prisoners have signed up for membership in a prisoners' union in that state. Further, he indicated having applied to the Delaware Labor Relations Board for certification of this union on the grounds that the prisoners are state employees. He anticipated rejection and saw court appeal as a next possible step.[21]

The Department of Correctional Services in New York State advised that:

An attempt has recently been made to organize a prisoners' union at the Green Haven Correction Facility. . . . Although the proposal has been made to our department, we have not officially taken a position on the proposal. It is our belief that pursuant to the laws of New York State we would not be in a position to recognize such a union until such time that the Public Employees Relations Board of the State certified that a proper relationship existed which would require us to recognize the union.[22]

The department anticipates similar court litigation. An Imprisoned Citizens Union in Pennsylvania is reported, but details are lacking. I suspect that these efforts at unionization of prisoners are germinal seeds that ultimately may find favorable conditions for growth in the mainstream of expanding human rights.

Whatever the direction of further growth of prisoners' rights, whether inclusive of strengthened councils, or of unions, or of further court or legislative actions, or of the pressures of growing professionalization of the correctional field at all levels, or any combination of these factors, correctional administration faces the inevitable need to prepare for accelerated pressures to encompass change, not only in the management of prisons but also in the more basic purposes of prisons. Perhaps a partial guideline to the future can be found in the statement of the U.N. Consultative Group on the Prevention of Crime and the Treatment of Offenders:

Use of the institutional environment as a whole . . . also reflects the growing tendency to make the offender an active partner rather than a passive recipient of custodial care. Reliance on prisoner committees and other forms of inmate participation are further instances of this trend. Its effect is to encourage responsibility and self-respect which are crucial factors in rehabilitation." [23]

NOTES AND REFERENCES

1. Civil Rights Act, 42 U.S. Codes 1963 (1964).

2. *Manual on Jail Administration* (Washington, D.C.: National Sheriff's Association, 1970), p. 42.

3. "A Model Act for the Protection of Rights of Prisoners" (Paramus, N.J.: National Council on Crime and Delinquency, 1972), p. 3.

4. *Cantwell* vs. *Connecticut*, 310 US 296, 60 S.Ct. 900, 84 L.ed. 1213 (1939) applied in *Everette E. X. Cooke* vs. *J. W. Trumberg*, H.J.S.Ct. (12/14/64), in *American Law Review*, p. 1267.

5. *Gerald Jackson et al.* vs. *Edward J. Hendrick*, Philadelphia Court of Com-

mon Pleas, February 1971—Term No. 71—2437. Opinion filed April 7, 1972, by Judge J. Edmund Spaeth.

6. *New York Times*, September 12, 1971, and March 3, 1972, respectively.

7. *Jackson* vs. *Hendrick*, p. 216.

8. Ibid., pp. 224–225.

9. *Holt* vs. *Sarver*, 309 F Supp 362 (1970) aff'd 442 F 2d (8th Cir. 1971) in *A Model Act for the Protection of the Rights of Prisoners*, p. 12.

10. *Bryant* vs. *Hendrick*, Philadelphia Court of Common Pleas, August 11, 1970, in ibid., p. 12.

11. *Jackson* vs. *Hendrick*, p. 69, citing *Landman* vs. *Peyten*, 370 F 2d 135 (4th Cir. 1966).

12. *Robert J. Landman* vs. *M. L. Royster*, U.S. Dist. Court of Eastern District of Va., Richmond Division, Civil Action #170–69–R; filed October 30, 1971.

13. Ibid.

14. *Johnson* vs. *Avery* (37 L.W. 4128) in Elizabeth Buttenwieser, "Prisoners' Rights" (unpublished paper, 1972, the School of Social Work and Social Research, Bryn Mawr College, Bryn Mawr, Pa.)

15. Albert Morris, "The Involvement of Offenders in the Prevention and Correction of Criminal Behavior," Bulletin No. 20, Massachusetts Correctional Association (1970), p. 18.

16. J. E. Baker, "Inmate Self-Government," *Journal of Criminal Law, Criminology and Police Science*, 55 (March 1964), pp. 40–41.

17. Roy B. Gerard, assistant director, U.S. Bureau of Prisons, letter dated August 18, 1972; personal interviews with Louis Aytch, superintendent, Philadelphia Bureau of Prisons, in July, 1972, and with Robert D. Kennedy, acting warden, Maine State Prison, Thomaston, Maine, on August 23, 1972.

18. Bo Martinsson, "Prison Democracy in Sweden," *Viewpoint*, April 16, 1971, pp. 1–5.

19. Norman Bishop, head, Planning and Development Unit, Kriminalvardsstyrelson, Sweden, letter dated August 11, 1972.

20. *New York Times*, September 26, 1971, p. 74.

21. J. Boomer, attorney, Community Legal Services, Wilmington, Del., telephone conversation, July, 1972.

22. Patrick J. Fish, associate attorney, Department of Correctional Services, Albany, N.Y., letter dated August 28, 1972.

23. "Report of the United Nations Consultative Group on the Prevention of Crime and the Treatment of Offenders" (New York: United Nations, 1968), p. 25, item III.

8

Rehabilitating Offenders Through Behavioral Change

Ellen Ryan Rest

IN THE PAST two hundred years, incarceration has evolved as the principal technique of punishment for public offenders. Before that, incarceration was not widely used. Instead, the fundamental goal of criminal law was vengeance, and among the punitive measures used were exile, confiscation of personal property, public ridicule, involuntary servitude, mutilation, and forfeiture of life: in short, an eye for an eye, a tooth for a tooth, a life for a life. The state did not institute criminal proceedings against the accused; instead the injured party or his representatives sought reparation from the accused. The state acted only in matters of public peace and safety.

HISTORY

Eventually, the state began to assume some responsibility for protecting society from recurrence of the same offense, assuming authority for prosecution of the accused, and carrying out punishments imposed.[1] The state, assuming that criminals acted deliberately and exercised free will, sought to repress crime through fear. Punishments became more and more severe; at one point in seventeenth-century England, capital punishment was invoked for 240 separate offenses, some as minor as picking pockets. Moreover, since the law did not restrict judges in their imposition of penalties, judges were free to sentence in accordance with their own individual views on the seriousness of the offense, culpability of the accused, and the presumed need for deterrence.

"Classical" Period

The wide disparity between sentences imposed for similar offenses raised a storm of protest in the eighteenth century. Now known as the "classical" period in criminology, the time was marked by rigidly prescribed and invariable penalties, a reaction against unlimited judicial authority. However, the philosophy underlying the administration of corrections remained that of penitence and moral reorganization of the individual. The offender was held to be completely responsible for his actions, having chosen to commit a crime (sin) through exercise of his free will. In 1847 S. J. May of the New York Prison Association proposed that the offender should be imprisoned "until the evil disposition is removed from his heart; until his disqualification to go at large no longer exists; that is, until he is a reformed man." [2] Menninger noted that when the Maine State Prison opened, the first warden proclaimed:

> Prisons should be so constructed that even their aspect might be terrific and appear like what they should be—dark and comfortless abodes of guilt and wretchedness. No . . . degree of punishment . . . is in its nature so well adapted to purposes of preventing crime or reforming a criminal as close confinement in a solitary cell, in which, cut off from all hope of relief, the convict shall be furnished a hammock on which he may sleep, a block of wood on which he may sit, and with such coarse and wholesome food as may best be suited to a person in a situation designed for grief and penitence, and shall be favored with so much light from the firmament as may enable him to read the New Testament which will be given him as his sole companion and guide to a better life. There his vices and crimes shall become personified, and appear to his frightened imagination as covenants of his dark and dismal cell. They will surround him as so many hideous spectres and overwhelm him with horror and remorse.[3]

"Positive" School

In the mid-nineteenth century the "positive" school of criminology emerged. Diametrically opposed to the classical position, it "rejected the idea of free will and contended that to a significant degree human conduct is determined by hereditary and environmental forces beyond the control of the individual." [4] Whereas the classical position had emphasized the crime itself, the positive school emphasized the offender, making a plea for treatment of problems thought to cause criminal behavior.

THE CORRECTIONS FIELD TODAY

Ambivalence between the classical view of free will and the positivist position of determination plagues the field of criminal corrections today. Legislators and judges urged on by segments of the public often take the position of "let's get tough with criminals." Laws are enacted that make offenders who commit certain crimes ineligible for parole. Prosecutors urge judges to "throw the book" at certain offenders who appear before them repeatedly. The general public, weary of property loss and personal injury, again becomes apathetic.

On the other hand, those who espouse treatment for offenders, with the goal of rehabilitating them to be conforming members of society, believe that the inequities in society itself are the major causes of criminal behavior. Such proponents include practitioners of the behavioral sciences and helping professions who profess to have considerable insight not only into the causes of criminal behavior, but also into the direction of a successful program of treatment. The dichotomy can be encapsulated in two principles: "let the punishment fit the crime" and "let the treatment fit the needs of the offender." [5] Neither position has a good record for reducing either the incidence of crime or the rate of recidivism.

Sentencing Procedures

There are three types of sentencing procedures presently in use: the definite sentence, the indefinite sentence, and the indeterminate sentence. Many problems of incarceration are common to all three systems. Not only is there disparity in length of sentences for similar offenses between jurisdictions with different sentencing systems, but great disparity is often found in sentences within a single jurisdiction owing to the latitude allowed to judges. If no formal mechanism exists whereby judges can remain in communication regarding time meted out for similar offenses, the result is anguish and frustration for the offender who finds that forfeiture of a considerable segment of his life has been in part an arbitrary decision. The goal of objective and equitable though not necessarily uniform sentencing has been elusive.

Although in recent years nearly all corrections professionals have emphasized treatment and rehabilitation rather than punishment, in most instances resources have been woefully inadequate. Most prisons lack even the facilities to keep their occupants busy in institutional maintenance programs, much less in educational and vocational self-improvement pursuits. Counseling services are sparsely staffed and sporadic. The result has been boredom, frustration, and restlessness, provoking many institutional uprisings over the last twenty years. The American Correctional Association's *Manual of Correctional Standards* states that the basic purpose of imprisonment is the rehabilitation of those committed by society. Moreover, many state statutes explicitly say that the department that administers prisons must provide an affirmative program of rehabilitation, although few do. Reasons given for the deficiency are lack of funds, space, personnel, and community resources—all quite realistic. Legislatures are notoriously slow to appropriate funds for prison reform. So many other things have a higher priority.

Changing Character of Prisoners

Even the character of the prisoners themselves is changing. With the rise of the Black Power movement and improvement in educational levels among all prisoners have come increasingly vocal and articulate spokesmen who make demands on the whole correctional system. Everyone, white, black, and other minority groups, is much more cognizant of his civil rights. Every institution has a growing number of "jailhouse lawyers" who have forced prison administrators to stock prison libraries with law books. Recently the question has been raised whether prisoners have an enforceable right of access to meaningful rehabilitation programs. "Where reason for commitment is need for treatment, failure to provide it violates inmates' constitutional rights. If rehabilitation is the primary purpose for imprisonment of adults, then prison should be obliged to furnish an inmate with opportunity." [6] This position has not been upheld in any court. Turner points out that imprisonment serves purposes other than rehabilitation, such as protection of society.[7]

Parole

Under all sentencing procedures an offender may be considered for parole prior to termination of his maximum sentence. This decision is usually made by the parole board or sentencing authority on the recommendation of prison officials. The board looks for evidence that the offender has seen the error of his ways and is determined to "go straight." The evidence may include testimony by a chaplain that the prisoner has attended religious services regularly, good reports from the supervisor at the prisoner's work station, and compliance with even petty prison rules and regulations. Especially prized by parole boards are insightful statements made by prisoners to counselors and group therapists about "working through" their problems. Thus under all three systems, someone must make the decision that the offender is "rehabilitated or cured." But how can it be known that the process has occurred if there is no rehabilitation program and no objective criteria?

Most people believe that the primary purpose of a prison sentence is to punish the offender and that a secondary purpose is to deter others from crime. Punishment is an extremely complex procedure; often the results seem paradoxical when, for example, the procedure seems to maintain the very behavior it was programmed to suppress. Correctional workers are all too familiar with the parolee who repeatedly commits new offenses that return him to custody. Indeed, this paradoxical outcome is an unplanned consequence of the planned intervention-institutionalization. According to Keve, prison is itself a cause of crime because it does not offer what a prisoner needs. "It unfits the prisoner for return to the free world." [8]

EFFECTIVE PUNISHMENT

There is no doubt that punishment can be an effective measure to achieve changes in behavior.[9] Much experimental evidence has been amassed in studies with adults, children, and many infrahuman species. Of course, many results with animals cannot be replicated with humans for obvious ethical reasons. Nonetheless, little choice exists but to trust the animal data with reference to humans, in the face of evidence already accumulated.[10]

However, maximizing the effectiveness of punishment with human subjects presents many difficulties, such as the following:

1. Punishment is most effective when immediate, a condition difficult to meet in the criminal justice system for a variety of reasons. Often months and even years elapse between the commission of a crime and the implementation of a sentence.

2. Punishment must be severe enough to suppress the rate of ongoing behavior. If the criminal justice system does not meet this criterion, it is not for lack of trying. At least in terms of numbers incarcerated and length of sentences, the American system of criminal justice is among the most ferocious in the Western world. For example, the United States has two and one half times the number of prisoners England has per 100,000 population, and here sentences are longer.[11]

3. To be effective, punishment must also be consistent, applied without regard to the individual's attributes or characteristics—a standard impossible to achieve in every instance of offense. The offender convicted of a crime quickly learns to regret not the offense, but getting caught, although he must state otherwise if he is to persuade the parole board to release him.

4. Punishment must not be correlated with a reward which maintains or increases the probability that the offense will recur. For example, a teen-ager may find himself repeatedly in trouble with the police; correlated with each event is a large dose of attention from his father, who is usually heavily involved in his business affairs. The various sanctions applied by the police, such as warning, charging, detaining, and so on, are not effective punishment for the boy. Attention from his father is presumably a positive reinforcer or reward, maintaining the boy's delinquent activities, with the sanctions that are applied ineffective as punishment.

5. For maximal effectiveness there must be no way to escape or avoid punishment. This has particular relevance for the criminal justice system in which offenders who have enough money are often able, through superior legal defense, political influence, and so forth, to mitigate sanctions applied to them. Offenders with limited personal resources are not unaware of the seeming double standard, even though all citizens have a constitutional guarantee of equality before the law.

6. To make punishment effective, the programmer must make some alternative responses available to the subject other than the behavior for which he is being punished. One of the side effects of punishment procedures is the generating of emotional responses. These can take many forms, depending on a number of variables, and may include rage, aggression, apathy, fear, and grief. Consider the numbers of publicized disturbances among prisoners in the last twenty years. One often hears of prison programs that make alternative responses available to prisoners. Such programs have included the writing and production of plays, singing groups (some of whom make recordings), participation in medical research (including donating blood and organs), painting (including public art fairs of prisoners' work), vocational training programs introduced by the private sector, and sports teams competing with teams from the local community. One is always struck by the degree of enthusiasm invoked in the prisoners, and one wonders why this force cannot be harnessed and used effectively by corrections professionals to reduce the rate of recidivism.

The kind and duration of sentence imposed on an offender have implications for the effectiveness of sentences as a punishment procedure.

It has been shown that under the indefinite and indeterminate sentencing systems, the effect has been actually to lengthen the period of punishment, both of incarceration and parole. Community supervision—parole —has become an addition to the time in prison instead of an earned reduction as under the definite sentence system. Increasing the time served has not been effective either in deterring prospective offenders or in reducing recidivism. Behavior functional for adapting to society is, in effect, being extinguished through long separation from society. The prisoner has virtually no decision-making power, and no control over his existence, at least for improving it. Behavior shaped and maintained by the institution is complete dependency and submissiveness, and is labeled "good adjustment." Paradoxically, it seems that the goals professed by those who support a more flexible sentencing system are better served by a rigid system in which a judge fixes the maximum penalty up to that allowed by law, and a parole authority is permitted flexibility. "The definite sentence provides greater individualization, does not overload our prisons with destructively long terms, and does not hobble the parole board with long minimum terms."[12]

But the question still persists under all sentencing systems: how will it be known that the offender has been rehabilitated, and is ready for return to society? Volumes have been written about the need for improved correctional facilities, more and better trained staff, modern equipment and supplies, and so on. Unfortunately, many correctional institutions are tucked away in remote rural areas, almost as if the very sight of the institutions and their occupants—society's failures—gives offense. More recently, however, public officials are planning for increased community involvement in offender and prisoner rehabilitation through halfway houses, work release programs, and new locations for small correctional institutions in population centers in order to utilize community resources.

SELF-DETERMINATION OF REHABILITATION

One way of determining when a prisoner has been rehabilitated might be to let the prisoner himself make this determination. Novel as this may seem, it recognizes that the prisoner himself knows most about his own behavior. The prisoner could set up a series of behavioral criteria for himself, and with the assistance of corrections professionals develop a program within which the criteria could be reached. Corrections professionals could take responsibility for informing prisoners about opportunities available in business and industry through films and reading material; outside speakers could be brought in for informal question-and-answer sessions. Tours of industrial operations could be arranged for small groups. A well-informed prisoner would be in a better position to set up realistic behavioral criteria for himself.

Although institutions do a fair job in promoting leisure-time activities, there is much room for improvement. Sports and crafts activities could be greatly expanded so that all could participate. Reading materials should be provided which will keep prisoners informed about events in the outside world. In most institutions this is forbidden.

Many prisoners are deficient in skills and knowledge necessary to "negotiate the system" under which the rest of society lives. How to apply for a job and to understand the intricacies of health insurance, social security, auto insurance; how to use public and private service agencies; how to establish credit, save money, make time purchases without incurring usurious interest charges; how and with whom to lodge a complaint of unjust treatment—these are just a few of the skills of everyday living that most people take for granted. Some prisoners may express a deficiency in the ability to establish and maintain satisfactory interpersonal relationships at many different levels— with the family, social peers, and authority figures and across racial, religious, and national groups. Such skills can be acquired in an institution, as is being demonstrated at Valley View, an institution for boys in Illinois near Chicago. The program is based on a point economy.

BEHAVIORAL CHANGE PROGRAMS

Some other interesting behavioral-change programs have been developed in correctional institutions. During the late 1950s, an experiment was conducted at the National Training School for Boys in Washington, D.C., which increased participation in the educational program.[13] Achievement measured by objective testing was noted along a number of dimensions. The program was maintained by a system of positive reinforcement in the form of points which a prisoner could exchange for an inner-spring mattress, special food, such as steak and ice cream, a private room, private study space, use of a typewriter, use of lounge area and recreational equipment. Cohen, Filipczyk, and Bis pointed out that the procedures of the project were based on immediate positive reinforcements and delayed punishment, whereas in the standard penal system, procedures are based on immediate punishment and delayed reinforcement.

In another program, titled "Achievement Place," three predelinquent boys participated in a behavioral-change program in a home-style, community-based, treatment facility.[14] A point economy system was also used. Points were exchanged for reinforcers that would be available in the natural environment of free society: small allowances, use of bicycle, television, games, tools, access to snacks; and privileges such as going downtown, staying up late, and coming home late after school.

Although a set of behavioral criteria was not established in conjunction with incarceration for any participants in these programs, it is evident that parole boards have been quite impressed with the accomplishments of the participants. Perhaps, then, a more equitable sentencing plan would be to make use jointly of a definite sentencing system and terminal behavioral criteria, with release contingent either on expiration of sentence or achievement of terminal behavioral criteria, whichever comes first. Behavioral criteria would have to be very carefully specified between the prisoner and the professional staff to ensure that the prisoner's goals were realistic.

The following is an example of a realistic program that was set up for an offender in Illinois:

Jim T, a 24-year-old black Chicagoan, was sentenced to the state penitentiary at Pontiac (Ill.) for five years for burglarizing a parked car. Jim is a tenth-grade dropout with no salable work skills and no appreciable work record. He has been a numbers runner and is "street-wise."

In prison Jim elected to finish high school concurrently with a course in auto mechanics. He puts in an eight-hour day, five days per week, with his time divided between the two pursuits, and receives academic credit for his vocational training. For recreation Jim is learning to play the guitar and belongs to a small rock band at the institution. Criteria for his release include his working full time for six months as an auto mechanic after receiving his high school diploma and passing a standard practical examination in his trade. Jim expects to achieve these goals twenty-eight months after being sentenced. The warden was visibly impressed with Jim's work on his car, for which he paid the going rate into a special fund to be used to purchase recreational equipment and musical instruments for the prisoners. Jim learned how to set his rates in his high school vocational mathematics class.

The St. Cloud State Prison, Minnesota, recently inaugurated an experimental system of "contract programming" in which "the behavior changes are translated into performance objectives, i.e., certain things which the individual must accomplish or demonstrate." Stipulation is being made as to which goals should be accomplished before release and which can be pursued on parole or work release. The program is based on two assumptions:

> [First,] incarceration alone leaves true attitude or value change completely to chance or worse. This the public cannot afford from any point of view, be it safety, cost or societal obligation. Secondly, no human being can be expected to act in a responsible manner or even want to do so without some degree of participation or freedom to influence his own destiny. Consequently, for any program of correctional "rehabilitation" to have any probability of producing real change in the offender there needs to be some provision for self-determination.[15]

It is probable that no period of incarceration with rehabilitation can be effective without development of means within the community to maintain the new behavioral repertoire developed within the institution. Thus the burden of maintaining the behavior falls not only on community corrections workers, but also on the community at large. The newly released offender must be helped to get established without having to struggle once again with conditions identical to those he faced when the crime was committed. The technology already exists; its implementation is perhaps more difficult. Although it is true that not everyone living in poverty, ignorance, and deprivation becomes a public offender, nonetheless, a disproportionate number do. Thus it seems likely that if society finds the means to reinforce and maintain behavior shaped in prison that is functional for living in society, this will be a major step toward reduction of the crime rate itself.

NOTES AND REFERENCES

1. Sol Rubin, *The Law of Criminal Correction* (St. Paul: West, 1963).

2. Ibid., p. 433.

3. Karl Menninger, *The Crime of Punishment* (New York: Viking Press, 1968), p. 71.

4. E. K. Nelson, Jr., and Fred Richardson, "Perennial Problems in Criminological Research," *Crime and Delinquency*, 17 (January 1971), p. 24.

5. James Robison and Gerald Smith, "The Effectiveness of Correctional Programs," *Crime and Delinquency*, 17 (January 1971), p. 68.

6. W. B. Turner, "Establishing the Rule of Law in Prisons: A Manual for Prisoners' Rights Litigation," *Stanford Law Review*, 23 (January 1971), p. 71.

7. Ibid.

8. Paul W. Keve, *Imaginative Programming in Probation and Parole* (Minneapolis: University of Minnesota Press, 1967), p. 38.

9. Nathan H. Agrin and William C. Holz, "Punishment," in Werner K. Honig, ed., *Operant Behavior: Areas of Research and Applications* (New York: Appleton-Century-Crofts, 1966), pp. 380–447.

10. Barry F. Singer, "Psychological Studies of Punishment," *California Law Review*, 58 (March 1970), p. 408.

11. Rubin, op. cit., p. 139.

12. Ibid., p. 141.

13. Harold L. Cohen, J. Filipczyk, and J. Bis, *A Study of Contingencies Applicable to Special Education: Case I* (Baltimore: Educational Facility Press, 1967).

14. Elery L. Phillips, "Achievement Place: Token Reinforcement Procedures in a Home-Style Rehabilitation Setting for Pre-delinquent Boys," *Journal of Applied Behavior Analysis*, 1 (Winter 1968), pp. 312–323.

15. Charles B. Gadbois, *Contract Programming* (St. Cloud State Prison, Minnesota: 1972; mimeographed), p. 1.

9
Rights of Drug Addicts

Kurt Spitzer, Barbara Kent

Social workers are particularly concerned about the impact of drug abuse on all aspects of social functioning, including the criminal behavior engaged in by many addicts. Invariably, addicts become involved with law enforcement agencies; this involvement includes many complex transactions between the addict, law enforcement personnel, and social workers as well as members of the clinics and hospitals that provide treatment and rehabilitative services.

The participants in these transactions have widely divergent roles, usually have totally different objectives, and utilize conflicting approaches to the problems at hand. Certain aspects related to this complex transactional process are of particular significance to social workers and members of other service professions. They include the following:

1. The rights of the individual addict to access and continuity of care and treatment under conditions that ensure privacy and confidentiality.
2. The conflicts that emerge when social workers examine the rights and responsibilities of the professional to his client, his agency, the community, and particularly the law enforcement agencies.

3. The need to reexamine the role of the professional worker, including a consideration of practice approaches or models that seem to offer some hope for effectively dealing with the problems associated with drug abuse and the impact of drug abuse itself on the social functioning of those affected by the problem.

4. The development of a perspective for the involvement of health and human services professionals, in conjunction with consumers, in formulating social policy.

The experiences of one of the writers as a student social worker in a drug clinic of a suburban hospital in the Detroit area highlight these issues in relation to two of her clients, Bob and John. The student's problem-focused model of practice was conceptualized and tested by faculty and students of the social work practice program at the Wayne State University School of Social Work, Detroit, Michigan, as part of the development of an educational design for teaching and learning an integrated methods approach. This approach involves the utilization by the social worker of a wide

> variety of interventive methods, procedures or tasks as these seem most applicable in the light of his assessment of the problem.
>
> Clearly, the problem-focused stance leads the social worker in many directions in practice, including social action activity and social policy development whenever feasible and appropriate.[1]

WORK WITH BOB

The social work services provided by the student to Bob began with a crisis situation. Bob, a heroin addict in his twenties, had been shot by a sheriff's deputy while trying to escape from jail, where he had previously attempted to commit suicide. As a result of his injuries, Bob was placed in a hospital, under custody of the Sheriff's Department. His acting out behavior was a problem to the nursing staff, who requested help from the hospital's social work service, hoping that through the development of a relationship with a social worker, with opportunity for meaningful expression of his feelings, his behavior would become less disruptive.

Bob manifested considerable childlike impulsiveness, a lack of ego controls, and an inability to relate more than superficially to anyone, including the student, who saw him frequently and provided comprehensive services. Social work intervention techniques included encouragement of oral expressions of angry feelings and later focused on developing more appropriate behavior patterns and helping Bob to reflect on the consequences of his behavior before he acted. Bob was frightened about going to jail due to past experiences in the army stockade, and he threatened other escape attempts. Dealing with these fears helped him finally make the transition back to the jail without further self-harm. He made considerable progress. His depression lifted, he developed greater impulse control, and related more meaningfully to the student. However, it seems probable that none of this could have been accomplished without intervention in the hospital and law enforcement systems to safeguard his "right to treatment." These interventions involved the sheriff's deputies, the drug clinic itself, and the sheriff's department.

SHERIFF'S DEPUTIES At first, the deputies who were guarding Bob's hospital room denied the student access to him. Later on, they stood within earshot near the bed during the interviews. Free, private access to Bob was granted only after the student got in touch with the hospital administrator, who interceded with the sheriff's office. Both these systems had to be fairly open for this to happen. Ensuring the patient's right to privacy became the basis for a trusting relationship.

DRUG CLINIC The clinic provides intensive interdisciplinary services to its clients within a three-month period. Limited staff resources do not usually make possible ongoing follow-up services beyond this time period. However, the clinic system was open and flexible when the student was able to demonstrate the need for long-term follow-up when Bob was transferred to a county sanatorium and later to jail.

COUNTY SHERIFF'S DEPARTMENT This system was open enough to allow weekly private one-hour interviews between the client and the worker during his jail term, and the undersheriff was also open to telephone communication regarding the client's progress. After these weekly visitation rights were established, a discussion with drug clinic staff revealed that seven other clients were in jail, either on charges of possession of drugs or of robbery to support their habit. In some instances, these charges were pending before the clients entered the program. They all seemed to need ongoing counseling with regard to the impact of incarceration on them and their families and for help in planning to resume family and occupational roles when they were released. Permission was granted for these clients to be seen as well.

As a matter of fact, much interest was expressed by the sheriff's department personnel not only in having the social worker conduct a weekly drug group therapy session, but also in providing group therapy for addicts when the new jail facilities would be completed in the near future. A good relationship has been established with the undersheriff, who is now participating in a medical-legal committee at the hospital and has given a talk to students at the School of Social Work on "rehabilitation of drug offenders in the jail."

Because of a flexible social work approach and systems that were open to change, direct social work services to Bob thus led to a series of interventions designed to make continuing treatment possible for him and for other arrested clients. Perhaps, in turn, this will help pave the way for better treatment for all jail inmates.

WORK WITH JOHN

John also came to the clinic with a problem of heroin addiction. He had taken part in a number of robberies to obtain enough money to support both his habit and his wife and baby. At the time the clinic staff did not know of the robberies.

John was unemployed; he had been a motorcycle racer and mechanic but stopped working when his habit increased. He was suffering from hepatitis and was severely depressed. His motivation was quite poor; he requested marriage counseling but did not follow through on appointments. He attended group therapy about once a month but was unable to stop using heroin even though he was in the methadone detoxification program. His self-image was low, and he would not acknowledge or take personal responsibility for any of his problems.

A double crisis precipitated a period of constructive growth in John. His hepatitis became so severe that he had to be hospitalized. In the hospital the physicians told him he had only a year to live unless he stopped using drugs and alcohol. He also knew that he might soon be arrested for armed robbery. These crises gave him the opportunity to evoke new coping mechanisms and problem-solving devices. His relationship with the student became deeper, which eventually led to the student's involvement on a broader scale, especially when she learned of John's arrest.

The hospital had been informed that a warrant was out for his arrest on an armed robbery charge, and the police were notified when he was discharged from the hospital. John coped with this arrest rationally and acted responsibly in obtaining personal bond, showing up for court dates, and attending group meetings at the clinic. The student provided continuing support for John. She helped him obtain legal aid, helped his wife make plans for the period when he would be in jail, and attended the arraignment with him.

John's arrest in the hospital heightened the student's awareness of problems related to the hospital and the legal system, which were seriously affecting John's rehabilitation. These issues included that of confidentiality, the hospital staff's responsibilities in relation to treatment of the arrested patient, and related issues of basic human rights. As a first step, she visited the American Civil Liverties Union and obtained copies of the *Know Your Rights* pamphlet for all clinic clients. She also informed her field instructor of her interest in working within the hospital system to develop procedures for patients who were either in custody or about to be arraigned. Fortunately, the hospital system was receptive, and the hospital administrator and physicians on the hospital's Drug Abuse Committee recognized the need to establish policy and procedures. Consequently, a subcomittee of the Drug Abuse Committee was formed and was asked to formulate recommendations, and the student was appointed to serve as the coordinator of the subcommittee, subsequently called the Medical-Legal Committee.

One of the first problems the Medical-Legal Committee dealt with was brought to its attention by a juvenile court psychologist. He had found that juveniles apprehended by police because they seemed to be under the heavy influence of drugs were required by the juvenile court authorities to have a medical evaluation of their drug usage and its probable physical and emotional after affects as a condition for admission to the youth home. However, hospitals are usually reluctant to provide such evaluation in the absence of any guidelines or procedures related to medical services to juveniles in public custody. The police are therefore forced to return them to their parents. Could the hospital's emergency room provide this evaluation routinely?

The Medical-Legal Committee was broadened to become a community work group so that it could better define this problem and determine intervention procedures, as well as establish a cooperative plan between the hospital and police for treating all hospital patients in custody, with the aim of protecting their rights within the requirements of the law. The Medical-Legal Committee now includes hospital administrators and physicians, lawyers, the directors and administrators of the juvenile court and the Juvenile Home, the county undersheriff, the city chief of police, and a police chief who represents all other police departments in the county. It is hoped that in the future consumers will be included as well.

The student continued to serve as coordinator of the committee as it developed county-wide plans. This involved working closely with the hospital's administrator and professional staff to identify all relevant issues and questions for subsequent review by the hospital's attorney. The present plan provides for the three systems concerned—hospital, court, and law enforcement agencies—to develop independently plans regarding their role in facilitating resolution of these problems, to be presented to the total committee as a basis for formulating policy and procedures.

As the first step toward development of the hospital's recommendations on policies and procedures, the student took major responsibility for formulating some basic questions related to the civil rights of the patients to be served by the hospital and the clinic.

Following are excerpts from the "Problem Statement for the Medical-Legal Committee" prepared by the student:

> This committee of hospital, court, and law enforcement officials has been established to help develop policy in relation to:
>
> 1. Patients who are under arrest prior to entering the hospital and are police or sheriff's prisoners and under guard during their hospital stay
> 2. Patients who have warrants out for their arrest
> 3. Patients who are not under arrest, but who may need to be in custody for their own and others' safety
> 4. Juveniles in police or court custody, requiring medical evaluation of seemingly current drug usage.
>
> Especially with patients in the drug program, trust and confidentiality are important: If doctors and therapists are seen as an "arm of the law," patients will not come here for help. On the other hand, we wish to cooperate with the police and observe the law. The following are some questions needing clarification:
>
> 1. What is the hospital's responsibility to notify authorities of patient's whereabouts when a warrant is out for his arrest? What is staff's responsibility to inform the patient when we have this information?
> 2. What are patient's rights to confidentiality when he informs hospital personnel of criminal behavior? Do we have any responsibility to convey this information to the police?
> 3. What medical records are confidential?
> 4. When a patient is in police custody, at what point does his medical condition preclude police interrogation?
> 5. What visiting rights are patients in custody allowed ?
> 6. What hospital personnel have unlimited private access to these patients?
> 7. What will the standard procedure be for arrest of patients? May this be done in the hospital?
> 8. Are there guidelines for the use of lethal weapons by police and hospital security guards?

The issues specifically related to the medical evaluation of juveniles for the juvenile home are related to these questions as well, in that a general understanding of treatment and responsibilities for patients in custody is needed before the hospital accepts responsibility for medical evaluation and/or treatment of arrested juveniles who seem under drug influence. Juvenile home staff need a written evaluation by the hospital's emergency room doctor of the patient's ability to be safely held in a nonmedical facility. This is in order to protect the youth from possible physical harm, such as possible overdose or severe withdrawal. It is estimated that 1 or 2 juveniles per week would be involved on a county-wide basis. The court and police have been in conflict over this matter, with the juvenile home sometimes refusing to accept such patients without such an evaluation.

Juvenile home staff also sees a need for such a medical evaluation of some of their residents who return from weekend passes seeming to be under drug influence. The home states that they do not have medical facilities to care for drug addicts.

The following are some of the questions and issues which would appear to be involved in establishing procedures related to cooperative work with the juvenile court:

1. In what case does the parent need to sign for his child's treatment? What happens if the parent or youth will not sign?

2. Who will guard the youth while he is in the emergency room? In some cases might parents be considered for carrying this responsibility?

3. How is a decision made that the youth is under drug influence and needs such a medical evaluation? Do the police or the court make this determination?

4. The court requires a statement from the emergency room doctor that the youth can be safely held in a nonmedical facility. What legal protection is there for the doctor in relation to making this determination?

5. What will this medical evaluation consist of? What tests will be administered? Is there any violation of the rights of the youth when the results of such tests are made available to the juvenile home?

IMPLICATIONS FOR SOCIAL WORK

The student's involvement in policy formulation and in the sociolegal arena could well be viewed as a rather unique activity for a social worker. However, in a society that increasingly has come to regard the provision of basic health, education, and welfare services as a right, to be provided in a manner that respects the basic dignity of the consumer, this type of involvement may, indeed *should*, become a major function of the social worker and of other professional disciplines.

Reflecting the changes in public attitudes in viewing health services as a right, recent years have seen the development of proposals by such eminent figures as Senator Edward M. Kennedy and Leonard Woodcock, to cite just two examples. In the 1960s a nationwide organization, the Medical Committee for Human Rights, was formed, consisting of "10,000 consumers and health workers—nurses, technicians, doctors, aides, researchers and dentists, whose 71 chapters work to establish quality health care as a human right, not a privilege." [2] Pamphlets have also been published to assure patients of their rights during their hospitalization.[3]

In relation to the right to privacy, the following statement by the Joint Commission on Accreditation of Hospitals appears to be of particular significance in determining future policies and procedures of hospitals:

> Every individual who enters a hospital or other health facility for treatment retains certain rights to privacy, which should be protected by the hospital without respect to the patient's economic status or the source of payment for his care. Thus, representatives of agencies not connected with the hospital, and who are not directly or indirectly involved in the patient's care, should not be permitted access to the patient for the purpose of interviewing, interrogating or observing him, without his express consent given on each occasion when such access is sought. This protection should be provided in the emergency department and outpatient facilities as well as on the floors of the hospital. The hospital, like the church of old, must impart at least some sense of sanctuary.[4]

REHABILITATION OF MAGNA CHARTA

Institutions concerned with the education of future members of the human service professions have the difficult task of finding ways to prepare students for such tasks as participating effectively in policy development, helping citizens to know their civil and legal rights, and assisting them to protect those rights. This will require, in the preparation of human service personnel, a climate that openly and actively promotes and endorses such a stance. As an illustration, a unit of students and faculty at Wayne State University School of Social Work, working actively on issues related to the delivery of health and rehabilitation services, drew up the following "Rehabilitation Magna Charta," which was proposed as a basis for the service and education design of the unit. "Realizing that rights flow from responsibilities and the individual is the active agent in the rehabilitation process," [5] they specified the following twelve basic individual rights:

1. The right to a restorative approach from the day of entry into a rehabilitation plan.

2. The right to a form of rehabilitation which involves active collaboration *with* the patient.

3. The right to be informed of the nature of the rehabilitation process, of risks and benefits to the extent known, and whether or not any aspect of the process is experimental in nature.

4. The right to attainment of maximum feasible or possible capacity (physical, psychological, social).

5. The right to expect efficient rehabilitation services leading to achievement of maximum results with the least amount of resources (time, effort, money) necessary.

6. The right to have rehabilitation carried on with minimum dislocation of the patient's or family's life.

7. The right to have rehabilitation in noninstitutional settings wherever possible.

8. The right to rehabilitation irrespective of age, race, creed, sex, occupation, imputed or actual criminal offenses, or by virtue of having advocated or worked for change in the provision of rehabilitation services.

9. The right to expect that the rehabilitation process will be free of any representatives of enforcement, investigative, or financial agencies unless the patient, without duress, approves.

10. The right to expect that the participation in the rehabilitation process will not jeopardize self-respect, civil liberties, or the over-all state of well-being.

11. The right to protection against incrimination, which governs the maintenance of all rehabilitation records.

12. The right to expect meaningful, fulfilling work as an outcome of the rehabilitation process.

SOCIAL WORK'S ROLE IN
POLICY DEVELOPMENT

We are greatly concerned about prevailing perceptions and attitudes within our profession regarding the social worker's role in social action and policy formulation, which somehow are perceived as unrelated to direct services to clients. Indeed, serious questions are frequently raised as to whether such activities fall within the purview of our professional roles and functions. A mystique seems to have developed around these activities which has the effect of deterring the practitioner from seriously involving himself in this arena as part and parcel of his total service plan in relation to his clients. Somehow the underlying messages seem to say that this is an area reserved for administrators and community workers, since a large body of knowledge and skill is required as a basis for these activities. Agreed, there is much that needs to be learned by the social worker in preparation for these roles, but preparation for the social policy area needs to be considered essential for every social worker as an integral part of his total professional education.

This, then, reaffirms an old but unfortunately frequently abandoned concept which views policy development in human and practical terms, and in the context of its meaning for the individuals who are directly affected by it. Indeed, in a period when individual rights and needs are so frequently disregarded and violated by society's major social institutions, we *must* begin the task of preparing ourselves for one of the most significant functions which we as social workers can perform: serving in the role of shaper and influencer of our social systems to help bring about a heightened degree of humanity and responsiveness to the civil rights and basic human needs of the individual.

NOTES AND REFERENCES

1. Betty Welsh and Kurt Spitzer, "A Problem-focused Model of Practice," *Social Casework,* 50 (June 1969), p. 326.

2. *Patients' Rights and Advocacy: A Collection of Working Materials for Use by Health Activists* (Chicago: Medical Committee for Human Rights, 1972).

3. *Your Rights as a Patient* (King Health Center, Bronx, N.Y.); *Your Rights as a Patient at Yale–New Haven Hospital* (Dixwell Legal Rights Association, New Haven, Conn.); *Patients Rights* (National Health and Environmental Law Program, Los Angeles, Calif.); *Civil Rights and Legal Status,* (Ypsilanti State Hospital, Ypsilanti, Mich.), prepared by the Huron Valley chapter of NASW.

4. *Accreditation Manual for Hospitals* (Chicago: Joint Commission on Accreditation of Hospitals, 1971), p. 17.

5. "Rehabilitation of Magna Charta" formulated by faculty and students at Wayne State University: Maria Phaneuf, Professor, College of Nursing; Betty Rusnack, Associate Professor, School of Social Work; Kurt Spitzer, Associate Professor, School

of Social Work; Sharon Klein, graduate student, School of Social Work; and Jean Luciano, graduate student, School of Social Work. An unpublished document of the Health Learning Center, February 1972.

The concept of "rights flowing from responsibilities" was formulated by Martin Kope, associate director of nonvocational services, and John Sullivan, associate director of vocational rehabilitation, both of the Detroit League for the Handicapped. Reference should also be made to "Government Medicine: A Right to Health Care," by Mal Schechter, senior editor of *Hospital Practice Magazine*.

10

The Healthy Community: Prospects for the Future

James A. Goodman

SOME ASSUMPTIONS must be made explicit: (1) it is possible to describe the important dimensions of the community of the future; (2) the future refers to more than twenty years hence; and (3) it is possible to divine a healthy community and to predict services needed by that community. One way, then, to approach the issue of the future is to forecast the nature of the population groupings and some of the major problems that will confront them and from that draw conclusions about the need for various health services. There must be full recognition, however, that the trends of today may portend much for the actual delivery of services in the community of the future.

CRITERIA OF HEALTH

The varied meanings attached to criteria that designate a healthy individual, group, or community complicate the process of determining when a community enjoys a healthy status. Data on mortality and illness are indications of the extent of poor health, but they do not show fully the health status of the community. According to the definition of health found in the Constitution of the World Health Organization: "Health is a state of complete physical, mental and social well-being and not merely the absence of disease or infirmity."

The entire environment in which a person lives helps him maintain his health or contributes to poor health in a variety of ways. Some of the factors that contribute to health cannot presently be quantified. Education, social environment, meaningful employment, recreational opportunities, for example, are known to be significant. But the net effect of change in any one of these or many other factors may be difficult to measure, and may in fact only become apparent after many years.

The writer's conception of the healthy community of the future rests on certain assumptions:

1.   The citizens of the community have a clear responsibility for protecting their health. Any health modes that are developed must rely heavily on that participation in all phases of development and implementation.

2.   All levels of government have a responsibility for protecting the health of citizens.

3.   Prevention of ill health is to be preferred to treatment after ill health occurs.

4.   It is not possible with today's knowledge to prevent all ill health. Therefore, it is necessary to determine those areas in which practical expenditures of time and money will be significant in terms of prevention.

5.   The delivery of preventive health services should be performed by a variety of systems: private practitioners, group practice, public health agencies, and combinations yet untried.

6.   The financing of preventive and service delivery activities should represent a combination of private and governmental expenditures. Health insurance should be so designed that it contributes to the financing of these services.

Current approaches to health care are fragmented and frequently do damage to these assumptions. The dichotomy between mental health and physical health further complicates the ability to plan effectively for the healthy community of the future. However, the writer is in agreement with Wilson:

> I do not mean to suggest that the distinctiveness of mental health is unwarranted or that its identity should be muted. In significant respects, mental health is unique. At the same time if we are to serve our ultimate objectives, all of us [workers in

health care activities] must develop new means for integration and coordination of our efforts.[1]

In focusing narrowly on a view of health care, two interrelated points will likely be missed: (1) there is a health crisis, which mainly affects the poor and the nonwhites; and (2) there is a health care delivery crisis, which now affects almost everyone. As Geiger suggests:

> The two crises are related, but separate. And both have their roots in the social order: the health crisis because of the determining role of the social order in health, the health care delivery crisis because our arrangements for basic human services both reflect and express our social structure and policies.[2]

MINORITIES AND THE POOR

With respect to social structure, changes on a community level are taking place at such a rapid rate and in such drastic fashion that the entire nature of community living is being transformed. In this context, the writer agrees with Geiger's predictions about life for the urban minorities and the poor in the 1970s.

Deterioration of the Inner City

According to Geiger, "the white suburban noose" around the inner city will be drawn even tighter, and it is not likely that blacks, Puerto Ricans, and Chicanos will move out of the inner city and thus find improved housing or better communities.[3] For example, from 1960 to 1970 blacks in Chicago's inner city increased by 35.7 percent while whites decreased by 18.6 percent; and the black population in Los Angeles increased by 51.7 percent. Along with this change in population was the loss of industry, jobs, and money in the cities, which at the same time reduced the urban tax base and the possibility of rehabilitating the core city.

One can expect continued deterioration and abandonment of housing, continuing removal of blacks from commercially desirable areas, and

> . . . continuing failure of federal programs, as exemplified by current policies which—with whatever good intentions—have simply enriched white banks, insurance companies and real estate speculators, defrauded the poor and made the Department of Housing and Urban Development one of the major owners of slum and abandoned housing.[4]

Consequently, there will be even worse crowding and even more people in the ghetto will live in substandard, dangerous housing. Higher population densities will bring about failures of supporting services, particularly garbage collection, and thus rat and insect infestation will increase.

It is a foregone conclusion that inner-city schools will deteriorate still further, despite "token increases of funding accompanying the revived 'separate but equal' federal policy." [5] Thus minority children will receive even poorer education, which will further decrease their ability to compete for jobs in an increasingly technological labor market.

Unemployment

The unemployment rate—now more than 25 percent for young black urban men—will accelerate as increasing numbers of young blacks reach employment age. The flight of industry to the white suburbs will intensify the lack of job availability for these young men.

Forty-five percent of all the jobs are now located in the suburbs, as well as 70 to 80 percent of all the new jobs created each year. It is expected that by the late 1970s the white suburbs will be the major location of all employment. "In short, the suburbs will have the jobs, the land, the industries, the tax base to support schools and other services, the wealth and the whites; the central cities will be Black, Brown and broke." [6]

Welfare

Welfare programs will be retained, but they will still be inadequate, used more and more to regulate and control the poor, and destructive of family and community life.

Most of the basic institutions in the ghetto will continue to be controlled from outside the ghetto even if communities do take control of some schools, hospitals, and health centers, since "the primary instrument of control—the budget—will remain in 'downtown' political and governmental agencies not as susceptible to pressure from the poor and nonwhite." [7]

Nothing stated here is intended to suggest benign acceptance of the policies and programs that will produce this poor quality of life for the community of the future. We must focus our efforts on political and social change rather than on the narrower conception of health and mental health. The poor and nonwhite must be provided the technical assistance that will enable them to construct a healthy community centered in their humanity.

LEGISLATIVE TRENDS IN
HEALTH CARE

Where does community health care appear to be heading? What approaches and trends can be discerned from scrutinizing the legislative scene?

Health Maintenance Organization Bills

A major emphasis in federal health legislation is on improving the overall system for delivery of medical care. Examples of such bills are the Nixon Administration's Health Maintenance Organization (HMO) bills (H.R. 5615 and S. 1182). Two non-Administration bills are H.R. 11728 and S. 3327.

In his health message to Congress in January 1971, President Nixon applied the term "health maintenance organization" to the forty-year-old prepayment concept and said that his Administration would support this type of practice to reach about one fifth of the population.

The HMO bills are based on four principles:

1. They propose an organized system of health care that would be responsible for providing or otherwise assuring the delivery of specific services.

2. There would be an agreed-on set of comprehensive health maintenance and treatment services.

3. These services would be available to a voluntarily enrolled group of persons in a geographic area.

4. The system would reimburse through a prenegotiated and fixed periodic payment made by, or on behalf of, each person or family unit enrolled in the plan.

Although there is no one model, basically an HMO is set up so that a patient pays one fee each year to a group of physicians for all his family's medical services—physician, hospital, emergency, and prevention—regardless of how often he uses them.

The concept of the HMO has grown from the success of a variety of medical foundations and prepaid group practice organizations in various parts of the United States that are now providing health care services for more than seven million persons. The current bills propose a program of financial assistance to HMOs already in operation and to groups ready to plan or organize new HMOs, whether the group is hospital based, medical school based, or a free-standing outpatient facility or group of such facilities. The bills vary in coverage, with the non-Administration bills being more nearly comprehensive in the services to be offered as prepaid medical care.

During September 1972, the Senate passed the HMO bill sponsored by Senator Kennedy. But the House of Representatives took no action on any HMO bill in 1972. Consequently, legislative action was postponed until at least the middle of 1973.

Administration officials continue to favor the planning and development of HMOs. Under the Public Health Service Act, which authorized the Department of Health, Education, and Welfare (HEW) to experiment with the existing health delivery system, a HMO authority has been set up in the Health Services Administration of HEW and has distributed about $15 million to aid groups that need funds for planning or development. About eighty projects are currently being helped, though no new projects will be considered until after a bill has been passed.

It is reported by the Administration that if specific legislative authority is granted, it is prepared to request $60 million to operate the program in fiscal year 1973. In addition, HEW is planning to guarantee loans totaling $75 million for the same period. The Administration has projected that by 1980, federal HMO spending will total $1.1 billion in general revenues, and there will be guaranteed private HMO loans totaling $2.8 billion.

While the number of HMOs is increasing and some planning efforts have begun, the failure of Congress to enact legislation, the growing opposition of organized medicine, and some indications of disaffection with the idea by the Administration, are hampering widespread development.

Child Care Bills

What is there on the legislative scene that can provide indicators of what the future holds in relation to the special physical and mental health care needs and problems of children? Late in 1972 President Nixon vetoed a day care bill on the grounds that is was fiscally irresponsible, administratively unworkable, and would weaken the family. He stated that because of the bill's comprehensiveness, programs provided by it would "duplicate many existing and growing federal, state, and local efforts to provide social, medical, nutritional, and educational services to the very young." Clearly, here is an indication that the federal government's guidelines for children's programs are increasingly likely to point in the direction of cooperation among existing federal, state, county, and community programs. The veto reflects a deliberate implementation of a philosophy of decentralization.

An emphasis on decentralization can encourage the development of symbiotic relationships. When such a model is utilized, resources and programs can cooperatively coalesce, without their individual identities being lost. The result, it is to be hoped, will be synergistic: cooperative linkage among programs will be more effective than the same number of independent programs and health personnel working at the same time. Perhaps such a model is almost a necessity during a time of rapid social change such as the present—a time when traditional ways of viewing health needs and health care are being challenged, a period when the expectations of the population for having its health-related needs adequately met are increasing more rapidly than society's ability to meet them adequately.

Several child care bills are currently before Congress. Two similar child care bills were introduced in the Senate in February 1972—the Nelson-Mondale bill (S. 3193) and the Javits bill (S. 3229).

The Nelson-Mondale bill is a modification of the bill vetoed by the President. It attempts to revise some of the provisions to which the President objected; for example, there would be a reduction in the number of eligible grantees, a greater role for the states, an increase in participation by parents, and a sliding scale of fees to be paid by parents whose incomes are above the poverty level.

Community Mental Health Centers Act

Part F of the Community Mental Health Centers Act (amended in 1970 and funded in 1971) further indicates the trend toward decentralization and cooperation among levels of government. On the basis of competitive applications, sixty-four programs around the country have been funded, totaling $10 million. An integral part of this program is the provision for collaborative organization and delivery of services by community mental health centers and other local community, child, and family agencies. The act was designed to facilitate innovative approaches to coordinating and integrating a spectrum of existing services for children. The focus during the first year was on the development of innovative programs through staffing of community services. Out of this effort should come models of preventive programs that can reach out to children in their normal family and neighborhood settings.

A variety of approaches is being tried; if successful, they will be used as models elsewhere. They include parent-child walk-in centers, prenatal and well-baby clinic programs, parent education, and consultation and collaboration with the courts. In several communities the local school system will share in providing the services, concentrating on high-risk and underserved school populations. Other programs will focus on day care and nursery school facilities and staff in an attempt to identify problems early and to provide early intervention.

In the implementation of Part F, the emphasis is obviously on collaborative organization among levels of government and among professional groups and organizations, with the federal level providing a limited amount of funds and community-level organizations providing the innovation and the follow-through to solve health problems. Obviously, in communities where the tax base has eroded, provision of resources and matching of funds remain problematic.

COMPREHENSIVE COMMUNITY MENTAL HEALTH CENTERS

The era of community mental health centers began in 1963 when President John F. Kennedy sent a message to Congress calling for "a bold new approach" to the problems of mental illness. Out of this message came the Community Mental Health Centers Act which provided federal assistance for the construction of centers. In 1965 Congress authorized additional funds to help centers pay for professional and technical staff members during the early years of operation.

Differences from Public Mental Hospitals

How does the comprehensive community mental health center (CMHC) differ from the traditional public mental hospital? Of course, a key difference is in the word "community"; the CMHC patient remains in his home area with as little disruption in his normal pattern of living as is possible. As a result, a center is generally smaller than a public mental hospital. Although a hospital may serve all or a large portion of a state's population, a center is apt to cover from 75,000 to 20,000 persons.

In addition, the CMHC is designed to provide continuity of care, permitting a patient to receive the type of treatment he needs when he needs it. No longer must a patient choose between hospitalization or no treatment at all. He now has the following alternatives:

1. If his illness is severe enough, he can enter the center's inpatient facility for short-term hospitalization.

2. If he can remain on the job with supporting therapy, he can enter partial hospitalization.

3. If he needs outpatient treatment, he can receive it at the center.

4. If he faces an emergency, he can receive services at any time during the day or night.

Thus a given individual makes use of whatever health care services he may need, whether it is inpatient treatment, outpatient treatment, partial hospitalization (day or night care), emergency services twenty-four hours a day, or consultation and education to individuals and group leaders in a community. These constitute the five essential services offered by all centers that receive federal assistance.

Relationship of CMHCs to Federal Government

What is the relationship between CMHCs and the federal government? Basically, it is concerned with specified types of financial support. For construction, the federal government may provide two thirds of the cost in nonpoor areas and 90 percent in poverty-stricken areas. Federal staffing grants cover the cost of eligible services for eight years on a declining basis. In such areas, this begins at 90 percent for the first two years and decreases to 70 percent in the last three years of funding. In other areas, support starts at 75 percent and diminishes to 30 percent in the last three years of funding. This kind of support is clearly designed to encourage communities to develop their own financial resources on a continuing basis.

It is obvious, then, that the CMHC movement is relying on the support and involvement of multiple segments of our economy. In many cases, the federal government supplies a large proportion of the initial funds and the local community picks up the burden with a unique local mix of financial and other support from its own private and public sectors.

Again we come back to the key word, "community." Over four hundred functioning mental health centers are already providing both comprehensive treatment for the mentally ill and preventive treatment in local communities. Where this is happening, it must be stressed, it is the community itself that is accepting responsibility for making mental health services available to all of its residents. Consequently, organization differs from community to community. The services are not always found under one roof. Sometimes the center is an entirely new facility; frequently it is a merger of or an addition to existing services. No matter how it is administered, it is the close cooperation within the community that results in services that fit local needs and capacities.

Community mental health services are still far from being the total way of life in the organization of mental health care. There are custodial services, exemplified in state, county, and local public mental hospitals and in private institutions. Their customary minor attention to treatment and rehabilitation is yielding to new trends in positive therapy, and major changes in philosophy and practice are taking place. At the same time, the organizational pattern becomes more specifically oriented toward the community and reflects more strongly the concept of comprehensiveness of services.

Types of Facilities

More than three thousand facilities are currently providing mental health services. Using the definition developed in a 1970 National Institute of Mental Health nationwide survey of all identifiable mental health facilities, a facility is "an administratively distinct governmental, public, or private agency or institution, whose primary concern is the provision of direct mental health services to the mentally ill or emotionally disturbed." Using this definition, the survey classified facilities into eight major categories:

1. Public and private mental hospitals.
2. General hospitals providing psychiatric services, with either separate psychiatric units or a general psychiatric inpatient service.
3. Residential treatment centers for the emotionally disturbed.
4. Outpatient psychiatric clinics: administratively distinct facilities whose primary purpose is to provide nonresidential mental health services.
5. Mental health day/night facilities: separate facilities that offer a planned program of milieu therapy and other treatment modalities; designed for nonresidential patients who spend only part of a twenty-four-hour period in the facility.
6. Comprehensive community mental health centers.
7. Transitional mental health facilities: residential services that focus primarily on the provision of room and board and assistance in the activities of daily living rather than on a planned treatment program.
8. Multiservice mental health facilities: facilities that offer more than one major service (inpatient and outpatient, day and night) and are not considered to be primarily any one of the other types of facilities.

All these patterns of providing mental health service are necessary, and in many instances these services can be pointed out with genuine pride. Nevertheless, it is too well known that none of the many different kinds of mental health services now in operation can adequately treat the mentally ill. Furthermore, the higher quality services are maldistributed and not available at all in some areas. Mental health services are not financially accessible to much of the population. Moreover, the services are not well enough coordinated with one another and with other health and social service systems to assure appropriate use of mental health resources.

There is wide consensus today about the need for a delivery system characterized as community based, comprehensive in scope, coordinated with other service systems, emphasizing preventive and early and ambulatory care, and accountable to the public. For developing such a system there is further acknowledgment on the part of most people in the field that the CMHC represents the best conceptual model developed thus far.

In operation, the typical CMHC does not yet deserve all the characterizations just listed, but it does represent a major advance over the delivery systems that preceded it and with which it is now coexisting— public and private mental hospitals, assorted outpatient clinics, and solo-practicing mental health professionals.

IMPROVING THE QUALITY OF LIFE

None of these health activities fully addresses the problem of providing individuals and groups with the resources necessary to expand their capacity to develop their own mechanism of care. It is essential to face this in the development of proper caring methods. Current programs tend to focus on funding issues to the exclusion of any anticipated outcomes associated with such funding. A statement by a HEW program analysis group on the delivery of health services to the poor makes it clear that any plan concentrated primarily on funding mechanisms for the health care system, without requiring major changes in it, would be futile:

> It is strongly felt that support for only *financing* of health services will guarantee neither improved health status nor equality in the receipt of health services by the poor. Indeed, a substantial increase in demand for services through financing programs without a concomitant increase and redistribution of currently scarce health resources can be expected to lead to inflation of health care costs and continued inaccessibility to services for many of the poor. Support must be given to improving the organization and delivery of health services for the general population and, particularly at this time, for the poor.[8]

Essentially, the argument calls for treating health care delivery not as an isolated problem, but in the context of creating other significant changes in all the interrelated areas that determine the quality of life for the American population in general and for blacks and the poor in particular. If black and poor people are to benefit from positive mental health, we must find ways of intervening in their dysfunctional living arrangements to prevent the development of full-blown psychosocial problems.

The varied meanings attached to criteria for positive mental health complicate the process of finding appropriate methods of preventing mental illness. Jahoda, after a survey of the literature, concludes that there are six primary approaches to the concept: [9]

1. There are several proposals suggesting that indicators of positive mental health should be sought in the attitudes of an individual toward his own self. Various distinctions in the manner of perceiving oneself are regarded as demonstrating higher or lower degrees of health.

2. Another group of criteria designates the individual's style and degree of growth, development, or self-actualization as expressions of mental health. This group of criteria, in contrast to the first, is concerned not with self-perception but with what a person does with himself over a period of time.

3. Various proposals place the emphasis on a central synthesizing psychological function, incorporating some of the suggested criteria defined above. This function will here be called "integration."

The following criteria concentrate more exclusively on the individual's relation to reality:

1. Autonomy singles out the individual's degree of independence from social influences as most revealing of the state of his mental health.

2. A number of proposals suggest that mental health is manifested in the adequacy of an individual's perception of reality.

3. Finally, there are suggestions that environmental mastery be regarded as a criterion for mental health.

It is fairly clear that these categories are but dimensions of the opportunities to interact afforded an individual in the context of his own social milieu. He is called on to observe and respond to some aspect of both the internal and external world. The extent to which he can do this and not damage himself or others is indicative of the state of his mental health.

COSTS OF MENTAL ILLNESS

However defined, mental illness has certain dysfunctional consequences. A person who suffers from mental illness is less able to perform his assigned social roles. As a result of this inability, he, his family, and society must pay a price.

Generally speaking, the costs of mental illness are reflected in direct and indirect ways. Direct costs include all the money expended in diagnosis, treatment, research, training, prevention, and capital investment in caring facilities. Indirect costs are more difficult to determine but include the loss of projected income and the maintenance cost to the family or surrogates as well as the cost to taxpayers through the caretaker agencies as part of the legitimate baseline figure. Whatever method is used to determine the nature of mental illness and the accompanying financial loss, it is obvious that the expenditures by federal and state agencies are real and substantial.

Figures compiled in a report by the Joint Commission on Mental Illness and Health show these costs in some detail:

> In 1956, the total maintenance expenditures, as reported by the Interstate Clearing House, for patients in public mental hospitals was $662,146,372. . . . These expenditures . . . are, of course, only part of the annual State expenditures on mental illness and mental health. They are primarily the expenditures connected with the operation of the State, county, and psychopathic hospitals. They do, however, represent the major portion of State expenditures. In addition, the individual States spend (1955 data) about $13 million for mental health programs.[10]

In addition, the federal government's expenditures for mental health and illness activities exceed $1.5 billion.

Obviously, these direct expenditures do not show the full cost of mental illness. The cost factors associated with the loss of productive capacity are translated into additional financial demands on family and other resources that are rarely figured into the formula used to plan for subsequent budget years.

According to the National Clearinghouse for Mental Health Information, the estimate of the overall cost of mental illness is well in excess of $21 billion. This figure includes indirect as well as direct costs.

The public policy leading to governmental expenditures is indicative of the fact that the nation regards health as a privilege, not as a right. We must all become aware that mental health and mental illness are associated directly or indirectly with the totality of health problems in the community relating to the psychosocial functioning of the individual and the family. As Goldston suggests:

> This concept of community health—personal and environmental— offers a practical approach to the administrator seeking to

organize and allocate his resources. It enables him to group health problems into manageable segments both for planning and implementation. . . . The breadth of this concept leads us to think in terms of the health of the whole community, not just the categories of the communicable diseases, nursing services, vital statistics, and maternal and child health problems of yesteryear.[11]

In general, this concept has been put into operation through the activities of various public and nonpublic health-serving agencies. That is, there is general agreement in the helping professions that this is a viable concept. The question surfaces around the nature of the content, the qualifications of the helpers, the cost factors, and the specific nature of the health care delivery system.

Aside from the need for clearer definitions of "optimum mental health," there is a need for coordination of the programs in health, education, manpower training, and other people-oriented services. The need for such coordination is seen in the private as well as the public sector of the health care system.

POSITIVE MENTAL HEALTH

If it is true that positive mental health is an outcome of physically healthy individuals interacting in an environment in which stress levels are manageable, then we must place the highest priority on reducing the noxious agents in the social and physical environment.

The specific factors related to positive mental health are largely acquired: the capacity for control over one's own human impulses coupled with the ability to assess realities with considerable accuracy and to act appropriately on this assessment; the ability to form satisfying human relationships; and the ability to learn and to use what one has learned in useful work and self-renewing play.[12] We must look to the opportunities provided for self-actualization in the minority and poor population groups that represent the high-risk categories with respect to mental illness and related dysfunctions. The importance of providing adequate social and psychological space for these individuals takes on even larger significance when we see the extent to which poverty and racism restrict opportunities for the development of positive views of the self and others. Prevention, therefore, is an ideal to be worked toward and not a state of being.

NOTES AND REFERENCES

1. Vernon Wilson, "Evolution of the Partnership between Health and Mental Health," in unpublished Proceedings of a conference on the Twenty-fifth Anniversary of the National Mental Health Act (Washington, D.C., 1971), p. 71.

2. H. Jack Geiger, "Health Services in the Concentration Camp: Prospects for the Inner City in the 1970's," p. 4. Unpublished manuscript, 1972. Health Science Center, State University of New York, Stony Brook, N.Y.

3. Ibid.

4. Ibid., p. 11.

5. Ibid., p. 12.

6. Ibid.

7. Ibid., p. 13.

8. Office of the Assistant Secretary (Planning and Evaluation), Department of Health, Education, & Welfare, *Delivery of Health Services for the Poor* (Washington, D.C.: U.S. Government Printing Office, 1967), p. 2.

9. Marie Jahoda, *Current Concepts of Positive Mental Health* (New York: Basic Books, 1958), p. 23.

10. Rashi Fein, *Economics of Mental Illness* (New York: Basic Books, 1958), p. 28.

11. S. E. Goldston, *Mental Health Considerations in Public Health*, Public Health Service Publication No. 1898 (Chevy Chase, Md.: U.S. Department of Health, Education, & Welfare, 1969), p. 6.

12. *Crisis in Child Mental Health: Challenge for the 1970's,* report of the Joint Commission on the Mental Health of Children (New York: Harper & Row, 1969), p. 162.

11

Health, Social Work, and Social Justice

Bess Dana

In the 1940s the World Health Organization's definition of health as "optimal social well-being" served as a particularly romantic-revolutionary spur to professional action. Today, the multifaceted nature of health and disease is well accepted, even if the concept is still not well implemented. Today, health as a right, a new combination of romanticism and radicalism, is now the rallying cry for a new generation of health professionals. It remains to be seen how ready the social work profession is to define and take the social action implicit in this new commitment.

The record of that unruly conglomerate of people and services that makes up the so-called "health and medical care establishment" is dazzling when viewed in terms of the accomplishments of biomedical science. In terms of social justice, its record shakes what has been called our "narcissistic confidence in ourselves," based as that confidence is on our "almost unlimited faith in man's ability to know, and by knowing, do." [1] Scientific knowledge, as the national health record only too vividly indicates, has failed to close the gap between the health status of the white and that of the nonwhite, the affluent and the poor; to correct for the uneconomic, inefficient, and inequitable use of health care resources;

to bring rational judgment to bear on the behavior of the educational systems that provide the manpower for the health and medical care enterprise.

Social justice, if it is to be expressed in terms of health as a right, has something to do with knowledge to the degree that knowledge illuminates the human possibility and heightens the human expectation. It has also to do, fundamentally, with values, with the beliefs reflected in society's priorities; with the respect for others expressed in programs and services; with the willingness of members of the health profession to give up hard-won professional prerogatives when they fail to promote and implement the public will and the public trust. Skill and method, with which the social work profession has been preoccupied for so long, must represent the reconciliation of this knowledge-value mix, expressed in new and viable partnerships with the consumers of health services and in new and changing institutional commitments and arrangements.

There is abundant evidence in the behavior of the profession to indicate its ambivalence about social work's relationship to the health field and the lack of clarity about the relationship of the parts of the health and medical care field to the whole. Not all the issues of separatism of physical and mental health have been resolved, either in principle or in practice.

It is possible to suggest a set of behavioral objectives for the profession of social work that will set it more truly on the course toward justice than does the present behavioral code. But social workers should not delude themselves into believing that the cause of social justice, whether in health, welfare, education, or corrections, can be met by reform in social work alone. The task is to acknowledge the multidimensional aspects of the move from charity to justice in actions that demonstrate the capacity to put differences to work in common cause.

DEVELOPMENTAL PERSPECTIVES

Any attempt to dicuss health and medical care as a cohesive social system asks for semantic trouble. The fact is that there is no single umbrella term for the variety of services, institutions, programs, people, and auspices that deal with the health potentials and medical problems of contemporary Americans. Even Millis's division of the world of medicine into the two subworlds of "medical cure" and "health care" fails to take into account such psychosocial entities as the half-world in which the chronically ill and disabled too frequently live out their half-lives; the never-never land of intractable mental illness; the "third world" of health fads, fakes, and folklore.[2] Nor does the division into subworlds, no matter how precise the subdivision, describe the difficult rites of passage into any single one of them or illuminate the obstacles that stand in the way of moving readily from one subworld into another as needs, wants, and circumstances may require.

Americans get their health information, their health services, and their medical care in strange and various ways and in a variety of places. The fragmentation and discontinuity of care—the expression of, and the breeding ground for, many of the current inequities in the quantity, quality, and distribution of health and medical care services—are often alluded to as by-products of the scientific and technical take-over of medicine.

Conceptual Themes

History tells us otherwise. Science has indeed perpetuated and accelerated a tradition of separatism in American health and medical thought and social action; it did not invent it. The current health scene reflects the interplay of three distinct conceptual themes—eighteenth- and nineteenth-century altruism; twentieth-century rationalism; and the emerging theme of ecology which attempts to muster the forces of science and technology toward enhancement of the quality of life itself.

EIGHTEENTH CENTURY It is important to remember that eighteenth-century altruism, transplanted to colonial America from Elizabethan England, was responsible for the development of four major institutional components in today's health and medical care establishment: the general hospital, the mental hospital, the outpatient department, and the public health facility. In the absence of clear-cut diagnostic and therapeutic goals, each of these institutions represented an expression of moral obligation to a particular population group. Thompson reminds us that the eighteenth-century general hospital, the current symbol of high-quality medical care, had as its "primary mission the care of the poor. Though not de jure concerned with any but the medical aspects of social problems . . . American hospitals, in the eighteenth century, were often de facto multipurpose social institutions." [3] Like the general hospital, the free dispensary as precursor of the present-day outpatient department originated for the poor. Notkin describes the dispensary as "the first battleground of a war that is still being fought. Is access to medical care," he queries, "a right to all people or a privilege to those of low income?" [4]

Like the poor, the mentally ill were singled out as causes for special concern by the well-intentioned—and well-off—citizenry of the eighteenth century. Guided by mixed emotions of fear and human decency,

the early mental health activists directed their influence toward removing the mentally ill from workhouses, almshouses, and jails, and placing
them in mental hospitals. Even that most democratic of social health
utilities, the public health system, had its beginnings in the development
of special hospital services for a particular group, in this instance
merchant seamen, for whom the first public health hospital was established in 1798.

NINETEENTH CENTURY This patchwork design of health care services
persisted throughout the nineteenth century. McKeown indicates:

> . . . it was possible in the nineteenth century to build a hospital
> anywhere and for any purpose. Hospitals were founded in the
> most casual and somewhat irresponsible manner: by the provision
> of a will; by the whim of an eccentric benefactor; by the design
> of young physicians or surgeons to improve their prospects; by the
> wish of a small community to have its own hospital. In such ways
> was the location, size and character of many hospitals determined
> with little regard for the needs of patients or for the fact that
> the shape of the services was being fixed for more than a century.[5]

Beginning rumbles of the scientific revolution had, by the late 1880s,
given new importance to the hospital as the preferred environment for
the treatment of the seriously sick, whether rich or poor. The ability
to pay for services thus began to emerge as a factor in the allocation of
hospital beds. By the late 1800s, "free hospital care was provided only
for the destitute and in limited amounts; most beds in the late 1800's
were occupied by pay patients."[6]

TWENTIETH CENTURY The rapid ascendancy of science as the dominant
force in health and medical care in the early twentieth century thus
built on, rather than established, a tradition of separation, segregation, and
special privilege as a way of defining and meeting health needs. It is
important to note that the so-called Golden Age of Science did little
to alter the old distinctions between rich and poor and between the
mentally and physically ill that had guided the allocation of the health
resources of the age of altruism. Rather, to the sense of noblesse oblige
and enlightened self-interest which had motivated earlier efforts to
organize and distribute health care services, science added a new and
powerful intellectual rationale for the maintenance of separatism and
discrimination as the stylistic motif for health care delivery and introduced
new criteria for the further splintering of health and medical care.

As McKeown points out:

> The approach to biology and medicine established during the seventeenth century—and accelerating in the twentieth with the explosive increase in the resources of the physical and chemical sciences—was an engineering one based on a physical model. Nature was conceived in mechanistic terms, which led in biology to the idea that a living organism could be regarded as a machine which might be taken apart and reassembled if its structure and function were fully understood. In medicine, the same concept led further to the belief that an understanding of disease processes and of the body's response to them would make it possible to intervene therapeutically, mainly by physical (surgical), chemical, or electrical methods.[7]

Acting on this "simplistic, mechanical philosophy of structure-function relationships," medicine inevitably began to "see the patient less and less as a person . . . and more and more as a somewhat fragmented collection of thousands of variables. Since variables are normally studied in very small groups, their overall interdependence may entirely escape notice, because it is too complex for normal rational analysis. Alienation, at the 'human' level, is then inevitable."[8]

Divide-and-Conquer Approach

The divide-and-conquer approach at the hands of science and attendant technology not only served to depersonalize the doctor-patient relationship but reshuffled and reshaped the institutional components of the delivery system and introduced new criteria of eligibility for health and medical care services. The displacement of the general physician by the specialist; the shift in the center of care from the home to the hospital as the appropriate environment for service, teaching, and research; the endorsement of departmentalization as the proper structural response to specialization; the classification of patients in accordance with their principal disease and their subclassification in accordance with disease stages; the development of categorical funding for both service and research—all had their roots in the translation of the structure-function principle into the language of health and medical care organization.

McKeown suggests that the difficulties encountered by psychiatry in accommodating to the constraints imposed by the definition of illness in terms of the structure-function relationship account for the persistence of the separation of the study and treatment of mental illness from the study and treatment of physical illness.[9] Whether differences in ideology and method are at the base of the organizational and institutional split between physical and mental illness, it can be fairly said that the dominance of scientific thought in health organizational behavior has done little to make the mentally ill patient welcome in the general population of the ill or to unite the causes of physical and mental health. If anything, disagreement as to whether a medical or a social model is more appropriate as the organizing theme for dealing with the problems of mental health and disease has served to fractionate the mental health-illness field itself into several opposing camps.

The Medical Center

There can be little doubt that the influence of the scientific method in health care organization and delivery has been greatly supported and accelerated by the full-scale entry of the federal government into the conquest of disease at the end of World War II. Indeed, the "Bethesda model" (the model advanced by the National Institutes of Health) as expressed through the university medical center perhaps represents the fullest flowering of the language of science as articulated in the organization and delivery of health services. Designed to implement the allegedly interrelated triad of service, teaching, and research, the policies and practices of the university center reflect the capacity of research to influence the content and organization of education for the health professions and the power of the research-education combine to dictate the terms to which service is defined and offered. Thus, in actual practice, the university medical center, while the principal source of the biomedical triumphs of American medicine, is also the principal agent of its persistent inequities.

These take the form of admission and discharge practices that are strongly influenced by the patient's value as a "teaching case" or "research subject"; the concentration of manpower, technology, and money on acute rather than long-term illness; inpatient rather than ambulatory care; curative rather than preventive and health-maintenance services. Even that select group of patients who meet the elitist requirements of the university medical center are subject to diagnostic and treatment regimens which tend to overlook the demands and influences of social circumstances on the cause, course, and consequences of illness and/or disability and impose a disease-determined set of behavioral expectations on patients and families in which a high value is placed on the patient's compliance with medical orders, and little opportunity is afforded for him to participate in decision-making.

As the principal recipient of the research and health care dollar and as the primary focus for the education of health manpower, the medical center has the power to shape and manipulate the scope and nature of services. This power is not limited to the doctor-patient transaction within the hospital itself. Attitudes toward the patient set in motion during undergraduate and residency training find their way into the practice of medicine on the outside. Whether benign or malignant, neglect of the preclinical and long-term stages in the natural history of disease as appropriate focuses for research and teaching diminishes the development of scientific understanding of the total health-illness continuum and devalues preventive, primary, and tertiary care as rewarding and rewarded areas of service.

Thus, few consumers or providers of health and medical care services have not been affected either by the stunning achievements of the academic medical center or by the limitations of the medical definition of illness that it has promoted and transmitted. In fact, the record of the health and medical care behavior of the consumer up to the 1960s is largely one of remarkable adaptation to the specialization, episodic care, and depersonalization by a system that promised—and many times delivered—cure of disease, relief of pain, and prolongation of life. The fact that this adaptation was achieved at high social and psychological cost has only recently surfaced as a serious threat to medical control of health affairs.

Equally remarkable have been the willingness and flexibility of health care providers outside the academic medical center to accept, with minimum protest, the right of the center to serve as the organizational model for the whole panoply of health services and programs. Thus, while mindful of the differences imposed by the nature of the population served, chronic-care institutions have struggled toward excellence by fashioning their services in the image of the acute general hospital. Community hospitals have sought to acquire the status symbols of the teaching hospital—the kidney dialysis machine, the cardiac surgery unit, the deep X-ray therapy equipment. The private practice of medicine has rejected its heritage of comprehensive family care in favor of acquiring the attributes and behavioral style of specialization. Even public health programs, whether at the local, state, or federal level, have followed the pathways blazed by the teaching hospital to compartmentalization of functions, services, and funding. For example, the U.S. Children's Bureau, in its long and distinguished career in the promotion and support of innovative maternal and child health programs throughout the country, was only marginally successful in maintaining a link between child health and child welfare. The extensive national network of medical services sponsored by the Veterans Administration clearly bears the mark of the clinical science tradition in its separation of medical and psychiatric services, in its heavy concentration on inpatient care, in its focus on the individual veteran. It departs from the prevailing clinical science model chiefly in the provision of chronic and custodial care as a matter of legal responsibility, one suspects, rather than preference.

Service for Neglected Populations

Services to neglected population groups among the physically ill and handicapped have been delivered haphazardly, prompted sometimes by the profit motive (as in the case of the proprietary nursing home and the proprietary hospital); by philanthropic endeavor (as in the case of homes for the aged and the chronically ill); or increasingly by the accommodation of public institutions to the pressures of demands (as in the case of the primary-care purposes that hospital emergency rooms have come to serve). By the very nature of variations in auspices, eligibility for even this disorderly and spotty array of services exists by the will—or whim—of the provider, not by the right of the consumer. Ability to pay, skin color, political clout, personal connections, and social class are some of the prevailing considerations that influence access to care.

Biomedical science, as applied to physical illness in the heyday of the 1940s, 1950s, and early 1960s, has thus been long on technical inventiveness and accomplishment and short on social responsibility. Its contribution to society has been strongly influenced by its investment in cure rather than care, except as caring affects curing. Almost the reverse situation has obtained in the field of mental illness. Here, there has been no equivalent dramatic biomedical triumph to match the conquering of infectious disease and no technical advances to equate open-heart surgery or organ transplantation. In fact, until the recent success in the use of drug therapy to control mental dysfunctioning, the laboratory has yielded comparatively few clues to the cure of mental disease. Physical intervention, through psychosurgery, has raised serious ethical and legal questions; electroshock therapy is considered, in many circles, the treatment of last resort.

Organization and Delivery of Mental Health Services

The field of mental illness, however, has far outstripped the field of physical illness in the application of theoretical understanding of human behavior to the organization and delivery of services. Forced by the public's fear and misunderstanding of mental illness itself to retain a custodial function, it has, over the centuries, evolved a science out of caring. Bloom points out that "one very early benefit of psychoanalysis was the humanizing of social attitudes in general toward the mentally ill. The consequences for mental hospitals were quick to be felt, both in the reduction of brutal and depersonalizing practices, and more positively, in the added hope that was injected into the atmosphere of psychiatric therapy." [10]

While these institutional responses to growing scientific understanding were first expressed through reliance on the doctor-patient relationship as the principal modality of treatment, Sullivan, "in his rebellion against the intrapsychic emphasis which he found in all the different schools of psychiatry [of his time], helped to turn the spotlight on the social context of mental illness." [11] His efforts to control the therapeutic environment in an experimental ward for schizophrenics constituted the beginning of what was to become the major thrust of mental hospital treatment following World War II—the conversion of the hospital system itself into a therapeutic milieu. That new drug therapies accelerated this process cannot be overlooked, but in the context of the creative and courageous use of professional knowledge it is important to remember that many mental hospitals threw away the keys long before thorazine and lithium safeguarded their action.

In view of the responsible way in which mental hospitals have exercised their social mandate to care for the mentally ill through largely public funding, it is surprising to find that, until the 1960s, prevention and primary care were left in large measure to the private sector. Thus, the treatment of emotional disturbance, in contrast to that of psychotic behavior, has been subject to the same strictures that accrue to any other medical specialty: ability to pay, capacity to satisfy the interests of voluntary clinics—the whole dreary list of criteria that make high-quality care a luxury.

THE CONTEMPORARY CHALLENGE

It is hard to pinpoint the exact time in the history of health and medical care in this country when the health field's limited definition of its social responsibility began to be seriously challenged. Certainly, the challenge itself was first expressed not in comprehensive social action, but in a series of relatively small but cumulatively significant changes in institutional behavior. The Case Western Reserve University experiment in medical education, which introduced such post-Flexnerian

portant new insights for clinical practice as well as public health intervention.

3. A new appreciation for, and support of, social and behavioral science research as fundamental to the understanding of the etiology, prevention, and control of social health problems.

4. The growing engagement of behavioral and social scientists in operational research relevant to the organization and delivery of care.

5. A larger investment of research talents in model-building and demonstration projects at the community level.

6. Emerging interest in, and support of, systematic ways of evaluating the quality of care, with particular reference to outcome measurements.

Health Care Practice

That education and research have moved farther in the incorporation of a new social mandate for health and medical care than has health care practice is perhaps inevitable. Locked into service-delivery systems, beset by worries about the rising costs of health and medical care, and discouraged by the slowness with which institutional changes come about, it is difficult to identify progress. Yet, in the space of less than ten years:

1. Physicians have come to accept—in fact, even abuse—Medicare as a fact of life.

2. "Family" medicine has been revitalized to the status of a specialty.

3. Prepaid group practice even in these perilous times is advanced as the model for the delivery of high-quality health services.

4. Consumer engagement in health care planning has advanced from being a necessary concession to an irate community to become an integral component of health care management, expressed not only in board membership but in the monitoring efforts of patient advocates and the publication of a patient's Bill of Rights.

5. Outpatient departments are changing both their architecture and their service structure in the interest of greater efficiency and effectiveness in primary care.

6. The self-serving expansion plans of hospitals are now subject to review by community comprehensive planning boards.

7. University medical centers have joined the community mental health movement with community medicine engagement in enhancing the quality and quantity of health services.

8. The erratic, physician-dominated behavior of medical care services within the hospital itself is subject to new management controls, with the growing application of system theory to the organization and delivery

of hospital services. Thus, the operative words in the new vocabulary of hospital life are "planning," "comprehensive coverage," "evaluation," "quality control," and "cost-benefit analysis."

9. Unionization is growing as the organizational style for hospital employees at the unskilled, skilled, technical, and, increasingly, professional levels.

In the field of mental health, the social orientation initiated in the 1960s finds its present expression in: (1) "the shift from a case orientation to a social goal and task orientation"; [12] (2) incorporation of mental health services into multipurpose health clinics; (3) crisis intervention organizationally articulated through "hot lines" and drop-in clinics in high-risk neighborhoods; (4) the expansion of comprehensive community mental health centers; and (5) higher priority for outpatient treatment and a continuing decrease in length of hospitalization.

It is sobering to realize that most of these important changes represent a response to changes in public attitudes that have been incorporated in public policy rather than a strong movement within the health professions and institutions themselves. In these uneasy times, which threaten to reverse the trend from charity to justice, it is crucial that we do not revert to our less-than-glorious past in the absence of prodding and support from external forces. The science of health, as new research findings demonstrate, is the science of human behavior and social organization. The prevention of disease and disability, whether physical or mental, is intimately connected with the conditions of human life. Thus a retreat from the vigorous pursuit of a social mission for health and medical care delivery is a denial of both science and society.

IMPLICATIONS FOR SOCIAL WORK

The implications for social work education, practice, and research in keeping the pursuit of justice alive and well in the coming struggle transcend that small band of social workers who have cast their lot with health or medical care institutions and services. Nevertheless, the members of the profession most clearly identified with health care organization and delivery have a special responsibility to lead in shaping and influencing the whole of that profession as a force in advancing health as a right.

In the judgment of the author, social work in the health field has not given strong evidence of its capacity to assume this leadership role both for its own colleagues and for the overall network of health and medical care services. The developmental history of social work in health and medical care too clearly resembles the developmental history of the general health field to provide much comfort or complacency as to the profession's strengths and capacities as an agent of social change.

Identity Crisis

Social workers entered the health and medical care nonsystem largely via the hospital in the early 1900s, bringing their own identity crisis which long predated that of the nonsystem as a whole. Traditionally, social workers have spoken of themselves as being part of, and yet apart from, the particular subsystems in which they were invited to serve. The profession's organizational behavior suggests, however, that its thrust for self-survival brought social work closer to the goals of the dominant profession, medicine, and the dominant institution, the hospital. Thus, while adamant in defending the status of social work as an independent department, social work staff has consistently been deployed in compliance with the organization of medical services. Aware of the deficiencies in the physician's perception of social need, such services have nonetheless, with few exceptions, been offered on a physician-referral basis. Gaining support for a clinical approach to identifying and solving problems from both the social work profession—itself greatly influenced by psychoanalytic theory—and from medicine, social workers have overlooked the common denominator of the task, thus diluting the power of the profession to suggest and influence system changes. Working patiently with their physician-mentors to modify their attitudes toward individual patients, social workers have too often confused modifying with mollifying.

Deployment patterns reflect the equation of high-quality practice with the hospital. Relatively few social workers in the field of physical health and disability have sought employment in public hospitals or public health departments. The standards in the former and lack of "clinical" opportunity in the latter have been powerful factors in leading them to avoid public-supported service. As in the past, the psychiatric field appears to provide the most favorable environment, within the broad spectrum of health and medical care programs and services, to demonstrate social work's competency and effectiveness. Social workers have worn their badges as "junior therapists" proudly, finding in their relationship with the psychiatrist a common body of knowledge and techniques that they have had far more difficulty in establishing with the nonpsychiatric physician. Thus, playing the game of follow-the-leader with the psychiatrist in charge has somehow seemed less of a compromise than playing the game under the direction of pediatrician, internist, or, most compromising of all, surgeon.

Teamwork Concept

In general, social workers have been strong supporters of the teamwork concept, although not particularly clear whether they should opt for its expression through role diffusion or role differentiation. Too often, they have settled for the honor of team membership without being willing to assume the responsibilities of independent judgment or to face the consequences of putting their "difference" to work in common cause as collaboration requires.

Relationships with Consumers

Social work's relationship with the consumers of health services has been a curious one. Caught up in the medical model of service delivery, the profession has tended to reserve the term "consumer" for that anonymous person who lives in a vague geographic area called "the community." Social workers are concerned primarily with patients. For many years, they described their own activities as helping patients accept and adjust to illness and medical care. In the post-World War II period, that concern was broadened to include the achievement and maintenance of optimum social functioning. Nevertheless, social work's activities have continued to focus more clearly on the tasks of adaptation than on either prevention or health maintenance. Relying heavily on a system of referral to other social agencies and institutions for the comprehensive services implicit in the implementation of social functioning, social workers have been frustrated to find that their services also have become fragmented, discontinuous, and too frequently inaccessible at times of crisis.

Social workers' relationships with each other as staff members are supportive to the point of being overprotective. They cling to a hierarchical structure of staff organization, closely akin to the hierarchical pattern of medical staff organization. Junior staff members thus have little opportunity to participate in decision-making and little authority with which to back up their differences with their co-workers from other professions and vocations.

Admittedly, this is a purposely exaggerated account of the professional deficiencies. Social workers have been sensitive observers of the relationship of social and psychological factors to the cause, course, and outcome of illness, physical and mental. They know the rules, regulations, and policies of the institutions and programs in which they work well, and need no outside critic to point out their limitations. Many patients and families have benefited from their interventions. They have stood up to both the hospital administration and the physician when justice and equity so demanded. They often represent, in the fragmented system of medical care, the only continuing, familiar figure. Their activities do attempt to link the world outside with the work inside. In public health as in hospitals, they have been "patient advocates" long before the role became identified as something different from just plain social work practice. While not distinguished as innovators, social workers have constantly attempted to improve the quality of their practice, admittedly without a heavy investment of energy in the development of objective criteria for quality assessment. Colleagues in other fields of social work practice have found social workers in the health field valuable pathfinders in the jungle of health and medical care systems and subsystems, clear interpreters of medical information, and responsible referral sources. Social workers in nonpsychiatric settings have struggled to maintain respect as competent practitioners of the generic art of social casework as well as being just plain good environmental manipulators.

Most social workers saw in the aroused social consciousness of the mid-1960s a long-awaited opportunity to link their knowledge of the inadequacies and inequities of health and medical care services with an organized public movement to bring justice to bear in health affairs. It was shocking to discover that the growing public insistence on better health care, far from guaranteeing a larger and more effective role for professional social work as an essential modality in comprehensive health care services, tended either to ignore its potential contribution or to consider social workers as apologists for the establishment. With few exceptions, the small cadre of professional social workers recruited for service in new and changing community-based programs were not drawn from the ranks of organized medical and psychiatric services. Even more threatening to the profession's self-image as expert in the understanding of human need and an exponent of social justice was the tendency of the new social movements to dismiss the entire profession as irrelevant to the tasks and mission of social justice.

THE FUTURE

Although more influenced by than influential in organized public efforts to rectify the patient inequities and inefficiencies in the organization and delivery of health and medical care, social work's initial reaction of defensiveness and hurt in the face of attack and exclusion is slowly giving way to constructive action designed to help the profession keep up with change in the fundamental nature of health and medical care organization and delivery. Whether social workers can move from being rapid responders to become active shapers of change would seem to depend on their willingness to do the following:

1. Move from a follower to a partner status in social change by

identifying firmly with the tough, demanding concept of justice. This means that social work cannot continue to serve two masters, the system and the people, unless of course help to the system is defined as making it more responsive and adaptive to people's needs, wants, and capabilities.

2. Shake loose from an almost exclusive preoccupation with the hospital as the radial center of health and medical care and address itself to the behavioral changes that will be required to strengthen primary care and promote the linkage of primary, secondary, and tertiary resources toward the goal of comprehensive coverage.

3. View cautiously the equation of the advocate or ombudsman role with being on the consumer's side. Social work must acknowledge the hidden danger that the institutionalization of such roles can serve to cover up the cracks in the delivery of health services rather than expose and eliminate them.

4. Revitalize the old concept of teamwork with the courage and knowledge required to promote collaborative action that engages difference in common cause.

5. Acknowledge that the right to health imposes on the consumer the necessity to acquire knowledge of the options available to him and on the social worker the responsibility to help him acquire such knowledge. The social worker's task thus becomes that of joining his capabilities as a professional with the community's capacity for self-renewal and goal fulfillment.

6. Face up to the redefinition of "generic" not as a weak synthesis of vague goals and methods but as a firm core of values and objectives pursued with expert knowledge applicable to specific populations, programs, and problems.

7. Recognize that the changing nature of health problems requires the continuing pursuit of new knowledge and new techniques as inherent in professionalism.

8. Put social work's energies to work not only in supporting universal entitlement to health and medical care but in assuming responsibility for defining the social components of such care.

9. Begin immediately to influence the factors to be considered in the current movement toward implementing quality control of health and medical care services under federal funding.

10. Recognize the threat that the present situation in the United States poses not only to moving forward in pursuit of the promise of social justice but in undercutting even the shaky, tottering movement toward justice as a goal.

Fundamental to the ability to move ahead on these tasks is the recognition that the way in which social workers' behavior toward themselves, their colleagues, and, most of all, the consumers of their services either promotes or impedes justice defined as "truth in action." Implicit in this overview is the acknowledgment of the thin, fine line between seeking power for power's sake and joining the profession's strengths with the power of the people.

NOTES AND REFERENCES

1. David S. Landes and Charles Tilly, "What Is History?" in Landes and Tilly, eds., *History as Social Science* (Englewood Cliffs, N.J.: Prentice-Hall, 1971), p. 6.

2. John S. Millis, *A Rational Public Policy for Medical Education and Its Financing* (New York: National Fund for Medical Education, 1971), pp. 19–45.

3. John D. Thompson, "Health Care System: General Hospital," *Encyclopedia of Social Work* (New York: National Association of Social Workers, 1971), Vol. 1, p. 530.

4. Herbert Notkin, "Health Care System: Ambulatory Care," in ibid., p. 524.

5. Thomas McKeown, *Medicine in Modern Society: Medical Planning Based on Evaluation of Medical Achievement* (New York: Hafner, 1966), p. 133.

6. Ibid.

7. Thomas McKeown, "A Historical Appraisal of the Medical Task," in Gordon McLachlan and McKeown, eds., *Medical History and Medical Care* (London: Oxford University Press, 1971), p. 29.

8. Bernard Towers, *The Influence of Medical Technology on Medical Services,* in ibid., p. 165.

9. McKeown, "A Historical Appraisal of the Medical Task," pp. 27–51.

10. Samuel W. Bloom, *The Doctor and His Patient* (New York: Russell Sage Foundation, 1963), p. 200.

11. Ibid., p. 202.

12. Martin Nacman, "Social Workers in Mental Health Services," in *Encyclopedia of Social Work,* p. 827.

12

Income Maintenance and Social Justice

Mitchell I. Ginsberg

SOCIAL JUSTICE is not an exact term, nor does it lend itself to precise measurement. Easy to support as a general principle, without specifics it is largely meaningless.

This poses an especially acute problem for social workers. As with other professions, perhaps even more so, social work has emphasized its commitment to a system of values and ethics. Fundamental to this system is a conviction about the basic dignity and worth of the individual human being, about the right of each individual to the greatest degree of self-determination consistent with the same rights for other people.

BASIC PRINCIPLES

If social justice encompasses these values, then it is clear that they are not at all reflected in current income maintenance policies, let alone current practices. Before discussing why this is so and what this means for social workers, it might be well to indicate some of the principles that are basic to any income maintenance system reasonably consistent with current concepts of social justice.

There are many possible formulations, one of which would be the statement in the NASW *Goals of Public Social Policy:*

> . . . a first and basic requirement in any program of self-fulfill-ment is the provision of an adequate standard of living as a matter of right for all Americans. For those whom this cannot be achieved by employment, there must be a program of income guarantee that assures such income at a uniformly adequate level and with payment provided in a dignified and appropriate fashion.[1]

The recent "Policy Statement on Income Maintenance" of the National Assembly for Social Policy and Development outlines five principles underlying its policy recommendations to ensure an adequate system of income maintenance in the United States. These include the following:

ENTITLEMENT   All citizens are entitled to receive an adequate income based on need and the most reliable objective standards.

UNIVERSALITY   A universal system of income maintenance should be developed that views an adequate income as the right of all citizens. This means a comprehensive, national network of programs that ensures a minimum level of living for all American families available through public programs which supplement inadequate incomes from all sources.

ADEQUACY   The minimum level of income must be adequate and at the very least be sufficient to maintain families out of poverty. This should also include provisions for standards to rise with the cost of living, increases in real income, and so forth.

PREVENTION   The system should provide adequate resources for indi-viduals and families throughout their lives. The aim is to prevent poverty rather than to do something about its consequences. This means devising programs that provide a regularized and secure flow of income with prime reliance on earned income.

MULTIPLICITY OF PROGRAMS   The best way to develop an effective system is through multiple approaches. No monolithic solution can do the job.[2]

There are, of course, other ways of wording these principles and, indeed, others that could be added, such as these two:

INVOLVEMENT   The right of clients and consumers to participate appro-priately in the formulation and implementation of policies and practices.

PROTECTION OF DUE PROCESS The development of policies and procedures that safeguard individual rights.

Just listing these principles highlights how little the current income maintenance system embodies them. With rare exceptions almost none of the programs comes close to meeting the criteria. We are all too familiar with the evidence for this, and, indeed, with the fact that, if anything, conditions seems to be getting worse. One need only note developments in the last year: cutbacks in inadequate levels of payments; forced work relief programs; drastic tightening up of eligibility requirements; modifications and in some cases elimination of some due process provisions such as fair hearings; the actions of Congress and the Administration; and the national campaign and election just held.

It is easy to deplore these trends and to condemn specific individuals and groups. But the overwhelming reality is that these principles just outlined, which are basic to an adequate system of income maintenance, and the concept of social justice familiar to social workers, have little or no significant support among a large majority of the American people. Public support goes to the toughest antiwelfare rhetoric and actions. If put to a national referendum at this time, any program of welfare reform at all consistent with the idea of social justice would be overwhelmingly defeated. Why is this?

PUBLIC ATTITUDES

The so-called frontier tradition, the misuse of the concept of the work ethic, the failure to feel any personal stake in a decent program of income maintenance, all contribute. In addition, there are the myths that shape much of the national thinking, which include these among others:

1. The belief that welfare is the basic *cause* of the problem rather than the *result* of the failures of other systems.

2. The belief that widespread fraud and cheating exist in welfare and that millions of clients are taking advantage of the taxpayers. Some cheating and fraud do indeed occur, and social workers make no contribution by claiming otherwise. But it is a delusion to ascribe the recent increase in the welfare rolls to dishonesty. What about the large number of eligible persons who are *not* being helped? Who is concerned about *them?*

3. The widespread conviction that there are large numbers of persons who are employable, especially men, who can but will not work. How many people accept the truth that the number of employable

men is small, but that large numbers of welfare clients want to work if only jobs and child care were available? It is easier and more comfortable for the American public to blame the clients rather than to admit the need for more jobs as well as adequate jobs.

Back of these specific notions are other public misunderstandings: that welfare clients are overwhelmingly of minority background—that they travel from place to place looking for higher welfare payments—that illegitimate children are a primary factor in the increases in the welfare rolls—that welfare payments are too high and welfare clients live too well.

Now a new one has been added—that increases in welfare are largely owing to poor management and administration! No doubt these programs could be better administered; no doubt those in charge could have been more aggressive in using up-to-date management techniques. But what has to be repeated again and again is that better management and administration alone will not in themselves solve basic social problems such as poverty.[3]

Unfortunately, these myths and half-truths have influenced public attitudes and official policies. Over the centuries it has been a time-honored approach to blame the victims rather than to seek basic causes of the problem. What then are the implications for the profession that the social work concept of social justice has little relation to income maintenance programs?

IMPLICATIONS
FOR SOCIAL WORK

The fight for income maintenance and related programs must continue because they are at the heart of social work's concern and NASW's priorities of poverty and racism. Although the prospects for significant progress in the near future may be minimal, involvement of social work is more crucial than ever, at least to slow down—hopefully to reverse—recent harmful developments.

For individual social workers this means being willing to work in welfare and related agencies even though there may be less and less demand from these agencies for professional services. Sometimes, and in some places, programs can be a mockery of what social work stands for, and the most effective means of protest would be to avoid these programs. Some professionals believe they can be more effective outside the system, where they can criticize and attack it, and hopefully improve it. But each person must decide for himself. Needless to say, it would be a disaster if large numbers of social workers abandoned public welfare agencies, however rational their motivation.

Becoming Effective

Both the social worker and the profession at large must recognize that the so-called dichotomy between policy and practice is false. What practice issue is there that does not have policy implications and what social policy position is there that does not have direct relevance for practice? Everybody does not have to do the same job, and legitimate differences in emphasis and approach do exist. But unreal differences must not be created. Time, energy, and resources should not be used in fighting one another while the real enemies cut back and dismember desperately needed services.

Most essential for the individual social worker and NASW is to become more knowledgeable and sophisticated about the issues involved. Who would dispute that? But how to accomplish it is another matter because the mass of information necessary to understand income maintenance alternatives and their consequences is enormous. Who has the time and energy even to begin to absorb it, and where does one obtain it?

Key responsibility clearly belongs to the schools of social work—one all too poorly met. Too little attention is given to the substance of some of these programs and their implications for practice. To say that the schools cannot do everything is not to deny that they can do much more.

NASW also bears a major responsibility. Its program of continuing education, its national committees and commissions, its state and local chapters, and sometimes its publications must make appropriate information available to the membership. Yet information that is not absorbed and articles that are not read will achieve little. Progress in such matters is not easy or quick and makes demands for people's time, energy, and attention.

More information would not necessarily improve social work's effectiveness. In issues of income maintenance, as in so many others, a lack of sophistication, an unwillingness to face the basic dilemma involved, despite a host of good intentions, all conspire against success in influencing public policy.

The dilemmas facing the individual social worker and especially the professional organization have been highlighted by recent welfare and health legislation, but the issue goes far beyond any specific bill or act. NASW can legitimately advocate and support the most forward-looking and advanced positions on any issue as long as these positions are consistent with its basic objectives and the beliefs of the membership. It can argue for model systems and programs, point out the consequences of the failure to adopt them, and refuse to compromise in any significant way. Although not the approach of the author, it is a legitimate approach, but the profession cannot adopt this stance and at the same time expect to be politically effective and to get legislation according to its requirements. Nor is it possible to create and join coalitions for effective action without a capacity for accommodation and flexibility. To be involved in a coalition and to participate in effective political action require compromise whether the word or idea is palatable or not. Allies and supporters do not emerge from nonnegotiable positions.

Dangers and risks are inevitable in compromise and in political negotiation, and sometimes the line between compromise and "sell-out" is a fine one; it is sometimes better to have no bill at all than a meaningless or destructive one. But these are matters of judgment and no hard and fast rules exist to prevent mistakes.

The matter of importance is to face up to the alternatives and their consequences. Only then can some minimal contribution be made toward achieving the objectives of social justice.

The issue of coalition raises all kinds of problems. For example, on social policy issues in general, NASW must always seek out and give the most careful consideration to the attitudes of client and consumer groups. To adopt a different position from some of the people who will be affected by a program should not be done without careful consideration. But a professional association worthy of its purpose must sometimes be prepared to take a divergent position, however controversial and lonely, if its members and leaders are convinced that this must be done.

Knowledge

Social workers need to be more knowledgeable and sophisticated about substantive issues. For instance, it is clear that NASW's position on work requirements for men on welfare differs from that of the overwhelming majority of the American people. That does not mean the position is wrong or should be changed because others disagree. Similarly with social work's opposition to compulsory work for mothers, to all forms of work relief, and to work provisions for men who do not meet requirements of suitability. But the work ethic for able-bodied men and their responsibility for their children are strains that run deep in the American people, including many on welfare. Whatever social work's stance, it should be based on thorough consideration and thoughtful discussion and not be, or appear to be, a political slogan. Incidentally, it is worth noting that the work requirement for men is basic policy also in practically all other countries, including Scandinavia and the United Kingdom.

Social work has been vague or even silent about many other significant income maintenance issues. For example, the question of income disregards and the negative tax rate is crucial to considerations about the numbers of people covered, the level of payments, and the costs of the programs. Perhaps social workers have not understood it or its importance, but can this issue go by default to the economists without some social work participation in the discussion and eventual decision?

Of course, income maintenance programs go well beyond public welfare and obviously include social security, the most important program of all. Why has the profession of social work paid so little attention to it? It may well be that the only real answer to the public assistance dilemmas will be to expand and strengthen social security with coverage of additional groups such as all children and potential workers who have not yet been employed. At any rate, alternative approaches must be examined, not only the profession's own conventional wisdom.

Another vital issue concerns the payroll tax provisions of social security. No more regressive tax exists, with the burden being heaviest on the relatively low-income workers. Why is social work not considering the alternatives? Is it because the social security system is so sacred that changes may not even be explored?

Even if briefly, reference has to be made to separation of services and income maintenance, in which services would be available to those on welfare as needed and wanted, but not required. Social workers would presumably be able to use their skills without the client's being confused about the worker's role. NASW and most of the profession supported this approach, in part because there are social justice implications.*

Some of the questions are obvious. Are services likely to be more or less available? What about the fact that services will have to justify themselves with respect to funding and public support? How is it going to affect the worker's relationship to the client? How may it change social work practice as presently known? What about the impact on voluntary agencies and what about the purchase of services? How does separation affect the concept of the self-determination of clients and participation in decision-making?

---

* I am one of those who for a long time have strongly advocated that services should be separated. Although I realize that more problems exist in the separation than might have been expected, I remain convinced that in the long run it would be in the best interests of both clients and profession. The profession must not evade the difficult issues involved.

Evaluating Services

The question of evaluating the effectiveness of services and all the welfare programs is crucial. Social workers recognize how little evaluation has been done; so does the public. It will be a difficult task with the possibility of unexpected, perhaps unwanted, results. Some recent studies do, indeed, raise questions.[4] But this issue cannot be avoided any longer. Now there is no choice. Indeed, there should be no choice.

Universality of Services

Perhaps the overriding dilemma that goes to the heart of the concerns about social work and social justice is the question of universality of services. It is all too well known that when services and programs are income tested and limited to the poor, they tend to end up being poor services. Experience also has taught that relatively high-quality services available to all tend to be largely taken over by the nonpoor and those who do not carry a high priority in the list of social work concerns. How may this issue be resolved? If services could be expanded indefinitely and thus be available to all, the answers might be simple. But that is not the way it is, and social workers must face this dilemma; otherwise the decision once again will be made without them. That may happen anyway, but it should not be by default.

This paper does not try to detail the specifics of an income maintenance program. Major progress against poverty means tackling such problems as health, education, employment, discrimination, and the like. But a recommended income maintenance program would include the following:

1. Transfer of the aged, blind, and disabled to social security.
2. Guaranteed employment, with the government as employer of last resort.
3. A federally administered and financed income program based on need.
4. Expanded social services. A federalized income system can be largely incorporated into an expanded social security program. This issue should be another top priority item for NASW.

It bears repeating that the present income maintenance program has little or no consonance with a social work definition of social justice. Even if the required changes were well spelled out, the task ahead would be overwhelming. Meaningful changes will require resources and public and political support far beyond anything known before.

Social workers must try to take leadership to bring about coalitions with a broader base than have been created so far. Some of the strongest opposition to significant welfare reform has come from people just above the welfare level, from labor union members and other workers, and from many ethnic groups. They see these programs as being at their expense and supported by their taxes. The challenge for social work is to develop programs that respond to some of these concerns without sacrificing the interests of the lowest income groups—the top priority for social work. This means coalitions of all these groups or common interests. Can social workers help find and define these interests?

There is no great popular demand for social workers to assume this or any other leadership role. In fact, the 1972 election and the words of President Nixon point to the contrary. But there is no alternative to admitting our mistakes, ceasing to make sweeping claims that cannot be justified, and concentrating on improving the profession's competence.

But enough of self-denigration, of personal attacks on colleagues and the profession, and of the constant concern about not being liked. Certainly many social programs such as income maintenance have not worked out as hoped. It is all too clear that little progress has been made toward social justice, and those who paid little attention to what social workers proposed now suggest that social workers are responsible for these failures.

The truth is that social work services are a contribution to people, that many are better off because of what social workers do, and that their record matches favorably with any profession. Some have charged social work with being a "vested interest" and suggested that social workers seek "honest labor."

Let us admit it. Social workers do have a "vested interest" in better programs for people and in advancing the concepts of social justice. They claim and seek no monopoly. All who seek to join a coalition for such objectives would be welcome. That, indeed, would be honest labor for all.

NOTES AND REFERENCES

1. *Goals of Public Social Policy*, rev. ed. (New York: National Association of Social Workers, 1966), p. 54.

2. *Policy Statement on Income Maintenance* (New York: National Assembly for Social Policy and Development, 1971), p. 4.

3. Mitchell I. Ginsberg, "Welfare: The Program Nobody Wants," *The American Federationist, AFL-CIO* (September 1972).

4. "Has Social Work Failed?" *Social Service Review*, 46 (September 1972), pp. 427–431.

13

The New ADC: Aid to Dependent Corporations

Jeffrey R. Solomon

CERTAIN basic premises have troubled the country's income maintenance programs since their inception. Public welfare is one income transfer system; other income transfer systems, in the form of subsidy programs, are also found throughout government. Despite increasing welfare roles and increasing costs of income maintenance and social services, there is evidence that corporations profit more from governmental subsidies than do individuals. Thus the taxpayer pays substantially less for income maintenance programs than he does for subsidies to industry.

PUBLIC ASSISTANCE

In regard to public assistance there are three primary factors to be kept in view: (1) the cost of public assistance; (2) the benefit to families on public assistance; (3) the work ethic myth of public assistance.

In June 1936, $4.24 million was spent in the Aid to Families with Dependent Children Program. In December 1970, the amount increased a hundredfold to $486.23 million. Old Age Assistance increased sixteen times during this period. Major increases were also found in Aid to the

Disabled, Aid to the Blind, and general assistance. Yet despite these costs, only fifteen of the fifty-four jurisdictions administering public welfare programs were able to pay a full standard of assistance. Moreover, the standard of assistance did not come close to what the Bureau of Labor Statistics estimates as a lower living standard, and in most states it does not even come close to the poverty line. Even when cost-of-living adjustments were made, the recipient of public assistance was still consistently given the short end of the economic stick.

In January 1968, the President's Commission on Income Maintenance was appointed to investigate the dynamics and problems of income maintenance. The Commission's report states:

> We have concluded that more often than not the reason for poverty is not some personal failing, but the accident of being born to the wrong parents, or the lack of opportunity to become non-poor, or some other circumstance over which individuals have no control. . . . ⅔ of the poor are children under 18; ⅔ are white; ⅙ are over age 65; and perhaps most striking of all, over ⅓ of the poor live in families in which the family head works throughout the year. Among the working poor the average gap between family income and the poverty line exceeds $1000.[1]

It is important to note that the poverty line computed by the Bureau of Labor Statistics is much higher than that specified by the President's Commission on Income Maintenance.

THE POOR AND WORK

The Brookings Institution made a social-psychological study of work orientations. By means of a series of questionnaires and interview instruments and following a pilot run of the methodology, the study made extensive use of recipients' responses. Numerous intercorrelations were made, refining the results. Reliability tests constantly monitored data. Baltimore was chosen as the test city for recipients' responses, with the cooperation of the local welfare department. Work Incentive Program (WIN) respondents were chosen from Baltimore, the District of Columbia, Detroit, Milwaukee, Seattle, and the San Francisco Bay area. According to that study:

> The plight of the poor cannot be blamed on their having deviant goals or a deviant psychology. The ways in which the poor do differ from the affluent can reasonably be attributed to

the different experiences of success and failure in the world. There is ample evidence to suggest that children who are born poor face discriminatory barriers to advancement in the educational and occupational worlds, which thrust them into failure much more consistently than their middle class counterparts.[2]

Common arguments for proposing a work requirement are that work is psychologically valuable for welfare mothers and provides a model for their children. The data indicate that even long-term welfare mothers and their teenage sons, though the sons have spent virtually their entire lives on welfare, continue to have a strong work ethic and do not need to be taught the importance of work. To encourage welfare mothers to enter the work force, it is necessary to present them with a chance to experience success in jobs that will support them. But realistically what are the chances of training large numbers of welfare mothers so they can support their families above the poverty level?

The study documented that women in the Work Incentive Program (WIN) who were terminated therefrom without jobs showed greater self-acceptance of being a public assistance recipient. The program's failure had a direct negative influence on their work orientation. The picture that emerges is one of black welfare women who want to work but who, because of continuing failure in the work world, tend to become more accepting of welfare and less inclined to try again.[3]

FEDERAL SUBSIDY PROGRAMS

With some of these points in mind, let us look at the economics of federal subsidy programs in general. A staff study of the Joint Economic Committee (JEC) of Congress, reported on January 11, 1972, began with a quotation from a 1958 JEC report on economic growth and stability:

> The economic position of particular groups or industries should be consistently reevaluated in light of changing circumstances. Whatever their initial justification, subsidy programs should be so contrived as to eliminate the necessity for their continuation. The broad changes which must be expected in our economy require frequent revision in the scope and character of these programs if they are to achieve their purposes. Failure to adapt the substance of subsidies to changing demands and opportunities may be expected to prevent most efficient use of resources in the subsidized activities as well as in other types of economic endeavor. Where this is the case the subsidy not only fails its

immediate objective but also imposes real costs on the entire economy over the long run.[4]

This key point is proved by many factors:

The lack of principles on how a subsidy works has kept policy makers and the public from asking questions that would lead to the facts about subsidies. This absence of fact hides the enormous costs of the overall subsidy system and prevents the evaluation and elimination of inefficient and unfair subsidies. An unfortunate cycle has been maintained: absence of the facts about subsidy precludes the development of a public concern that would insist that these programs be carefully analyzed; and the lack of any readily available analytical framework makes it difficult to develop the appropriate facts. The result has been that Federal subsidy programs are maintained indefinitely and piled up one on top of another.

In all candor it should be acknowledged that use of the subsidy device as a political instrument has also contributed to our lack of knowledge about it. It appears that politically one needs only to support a program that seems to provide assistance to the special group seeking aid. The political incentives are to keep the argument for assistance vague and simple, making many references to the national interest, few references to careful economic analysis, and preferably not even referring to the assistance as a subsidy.[5]

Definitions

What is a subsidy? Hubbel defines it as follows:

A government or financial device which enables sellers to get more money or buyers to get more goods and services than would be the case if the affected commercial transactions had occurred without Government intervention. The financial device may involve: (1) direct or indirect payments in cash or kind; (2) provisions of goods or service for prices or fees which do not reflect full competitive market value; or (3) lower taxes which are exceptions to general tax rates.[6]

The Department of Commerce uses the following definition:

Monetary payments provided by government to private resident businesses including farms. Subsidies are excluded from government purchase of goods and services because they are not payments for any output, and they appear nowhere else in gross

national product. However, subsidies are considered as a portion
of currently earned private income and as such they appear in the
national income.[7]

The ubiquitous Office of Management and Budget refers to subsidy
in its definition of grants, subsidies, and contributions thus:

> Comprises grants, subsidies, gratuities and other aid for which
> cash payments are made to states, other political subdivisions,
> corporations, associations, or projects, whether in lump sum or
> as quota of expenses; contributions fixed by treaty; grants to
> foreign countries; taxes imposed by taxing authorities where the
> Federal government has consented to taxation; and payments in
> lieu of taxes.

A classic example of differing definitions may be found in the testimony relating to the government guarantee of $250 million to Lockeed
Aircraft Corporation:

> SENATOR PROXMIRE: You raise a very profound economic ques-
> tion. One that it seems to me we ought to have the best
> economic advice we can get.
>   I have written to a number of economists, about 20, and
> only one indicated he favors this. The rest of them over-
> whelmingly indicated that they oppose the Lockheed guar-
> antee.
>   . . . What bothers me so much about this, Mr. Secretary,
> is that Lockheed's bail out, I would agree with Senator
> Tower, is not a subsidy. It is different from a subsidy, it is
> the beginning of a welfare program for large corporations.
>   I would remind you in a subsidy program it is different.
> There is a quid pro quo. You make a payment to a railroad
> in return they do a trackage; you make a payment to an
> airline and they provide a certain amount of service for it.
>   In welfare, of course, you make a payment and there is no
> return. In this case we have a guarantee and there is no
> requirement on the part of Lockheed to perform under that
> guarantee. A guarantee of $250 million and no benefit, no
> pro quo.
> SECRETARY CONNALLY: What do you mean no benefit?
> SENATOR PROXMIRE: Well, they do not have to perform.
> SECRETARY CONNALLY: What do we care whether they perform?

> We are guaranteeing them basically a $250 million loan. What for? Basically so they can hopefully minimize their losses so they can provide employment for 31,000 people throughout the country at a time when we desperately need that type of employment. That is basically a rationale and justification.
>
> SENATOR PROXMIRE: Exactly. That is the welfare rationale, precisely as we give food stamps to a hungry family, because we do not want them to starve. But they do not have to perform for us, there is no benefit.[8]

A definition of subsidy as agreed to by the JEC study is considerably different from that of Senator Proxmire. Many subsidy programs now, like the loan to Lockheed, do not return anything for those dollars. Others do not provide the positive cost benefits to government that social workers have increasingly learned they must provide. For example, the shipping industry, owing to the generosity of the federal government, is required to pay merchant marines only a foreign wage rate. Merchant marines cannot work at foreign wage rates. They earn from $16,000 to $30,000 annually. The average merchant marine is paid $4,000 per year by the shipping company; the U.S. government supplements that income by over $12,000 annually.[9]

Economist Schultz, budget director under President Johnson, has completed perhaps the first precise measurement of the effects of a $10 billion distribution of farm-income transfers. He shows that the wealthiest 7 percent of farm families receive federal benefits averaging $14,000 (raising their net farm income from $13,400 to $27,500), while the poorest 40 percent receive an average benefit of $300 (boosting them to a net farm income of $1,100). Schultz also calculates that the poorer half of the farm population receives 9.1 percent of the total federal subsidy, while the wealthiest 19 percent takes home 62.8 percent of the federal money.[10]

A further outrage relates specifically to the current Administration:

> In the Revenue Act of 1971, President Nixon pushed through his proposals for adding the largest single boost to the parade of commerce subsidies in more than 40 years—$6 billion a year in tax credits and accelerated depreciation for corporations, which amounted to 10 percent in corporate taxes.[11]

These gains are felt only by the large major corporations that are in capital positions to take advantage of the write-offs. This must be viewed against the fact that the $4 billion family assistance program was not pushed through Congress.

Types of Subsidy

The JEC study concludes that there are five categories of subsidy. Unfortunately, not even the staff of Congress can estimate the true cost to the taxpayer of these five categories. They are able to say that it is significantly over $63 billion. Public assistance expenditures represent only $10 billion of that $62 billion plus. Specifically, the six categories of subsidy are these:

Federal cash payment subsidies that include direct cash programs, such as those relating to commodity purchases and agriculture, construction, training, and medical care; work incentive, vocational rehabilitation, and manpower; a variety of programs in education; export payments and international trade; rent supplements and rehabilitation grants for housing; assistance programs for the environment; air carrier payments and subsidies, transportation, and a number of commercial and economic development programs. It is estimated that $11.8 billion is spent in this manner. This may be compared to the $38.4 billion that the government subsidizes each year through tax deductions. Of that $38.4 billion, the amount deductible for charitable contributions is only $3.4 billion, as compared to the $7.5 billion deductible for capital gains.

Tax subsidies represent the chief means of noncash subsidy provided by the federal government. The tax reduction "is limited to those who produce, purchase, or sell certain specified types of goods or factors of production. It is a selective tax relief that is not found in the law drafted for taxpayers in general." [12] For example, the investment credit of the 1960s was an instance of subsidy through tax reduction. Purchasers of long-lived machinery could subtract from tax otherwise due an amount equal to 7 percent of what they paid for the capital goods.

Government credit programs represent a major category for which estimates of gross outlays cannot even be made. These are highlighted by price-support loans, export financing, student loans, and international development loans. The Office of Management and Budget estimates that direct and guaranteed loans outstanding grossly total $224 billion. [13]

Benefit-in-kind subsidies represent another category in which estimates are virtually impossible to make. We know that the direct programs cost no less than $9.2 billion annually. These are programs in which the government sells the private sector goods or services at a price below market value and below cost when there is no readily discernible private market. Examples are the federal airways system, the rural water and waste disposal system, the food stamp program, and the postal service. In addition, accounting practices might call for the sector that derives the benefit of certain federal regulatory agencies to pay for those costs. It is here that it is impossible to make subsidy estimates.

For example, while it costs the Department of Agriculture $2.32 billion to inspect and grade grain grown in the United States, the department collects only $919 million for this service. Similarly, the Civil Aeronautics Board spends $2,758 million on licensing pilots; it collects only $689.4 million in fees.[14]

Purchase subsidies occur when the government deliberately purchases goods or services from the private sector at a higher price than it would have to pay on the market. No cost estimates are given, but the JEC report says that little is known about such governmental purchases, their extent or cost, or their effect on private markets.[15]

The experience in procurement by the Defense Department, however, seems to indicate that such subsidies are pervasive and that extensive public investigations to determine the scope and effects of this subsidy form are merited.

Regulatory subsidies are those in which regulatory authorities of government permit price-gouging on specific items or in geographic areas to make up for losses that industry may be suffering on other items or in other geographic areas. Total costs are not known. According to the report: "There is no more known about this subsidy form than Purchase Subsidies, and consequently they are not accounted for in the study. There are indications that the cost of these subsidies is extremely large." [16] It is estimated that the cost of the oil import quota subsidy alone is approximately five million dollars.[17]

CONCLUSION

What does this documentation prove? It again supports the conviction that corporations obtain substantially more benefits from government than individuals. Clearly, that is not news. We must look toward achieving an income maintenance system that provides equity and adequacy in the same terms applied to private industry. Our legislators must be asked why a merchant marine earning $16,000 to $30,000 a year must get a government subsidy four to five times as large as that provided to a family who cannot find work. The time for radical tax reform is here, and the public welfare advocate must be aware of what reforms are needed and how best to achieve them.

Social workers can no longer feel comfortable with merely knowing a great deal about the dynamics of human development. Now that income maintenance is separated from social services, social workers who remain in public welfare systems must become experts in income maintenance as an income transfer service and in the economics of governmental payment systems just as they were once experts in the dynamics of normal and deviant behavior. The "anality" of the federal government industrial fiscal relationships must now be moved toward the "genitality" of equity and adequacy for government beneficiaries, regardless of corporate status and including those beneficiaries who are the consumers of the public welfare system.

NOTES AND REFERENCES

1. President's Commission on Income Maintenance Programs, *Poverty Amid Plenty: the American Paradox* (Washington, D.C.: U.S. Government Printing Office, 1969), pp. 2–3.

2. Leonard Goodwin, *Do the Poor Want to Go to Work?* (Washington, D.C.: Brookings Institute, 1972), p. 118.

3. Ibid., p. 113.

4. Joint Economic Committee, United States Congress, *Report of the Subcommittee on Fiscal Policy on Federal Expenditure Policies for Economic Growth and Stability* (Washington, D.C.: U.S. Government Printing Office, 1958), p. 1.

5. Joint Economic Committee, United States Congress, *The Economics of Federal Subsidy Programs* (Washington, D.C.: U.S. Government Printing Office, 1972), p. 2.

6. Robert Hubbell, "Concealed Subsidies in the Federal Budget," *National Tax Journal*, September 1957, p. 215, as reported in ibid., p. 9.

7. Office of Business Economics, Department of Commerce, as reported in *The Economics of Federal Subsidy Programs*, p. 10.

8. Joint Economic Committee, *Report*, p. 16.

9. Taylor Branch, "Government Subsidies: Who Gets the $62 Billion?" *Washington Monthly*, March 1972, p. 16.

10. Charles Schultz, as reported in ibid., p. 12.

11. Ibid., p. 18.

12. Joint Economic Committee, *Report*, p. 26.

13. Ibid., p. 31.

14. Ibid., p. 34.

15. Ibid., p. 38.

16. Ibid.

17. Ibid., p. 40.

14

Professional Dilemmas

Bernard Ross

SOCIAL JUSTICE is not merely what one does for others; essentially it is what one does for oneself—not as a quid pro quo but in terms of the capacity to identify values and live by them. In the Bible, social justice is concerned with man's salvation; it is an active process of *being personally involved* in the community. Although social justice is concerned with others and particularly those in special jeopardy—prisoners, patients, pupils, poor people—its source is concern for oneself. It begins with the question: "How will *I* survive in a world where this can happen to other people? If it happens to them, can it happen to *me?*"

It is largely believed that social workers choose their profession because they seek self-fulfillment through service to others. Thus it is not surprising that they view their profession as fundamentally concerned with social justice.

In this twentieth-century world in which the individual lives through group associations, contractual relationships, and reciprocal role relationships—in other words, in a mass society—the social work profession has for, better or worse, transformed these individual urges toward self-fulfillment into a collective conscience. The reason is that to be effective, the individual social worker can hardly find "salvation" by individualistic means. He must relate to many existing systems—his profession, a service system, an educational system, a system of government. He has limited control over his own destiny, let alone the destiny of those for whom he claims professional concern. He must constantly ask himself: To what end my professional activity? Will what I am doing actually help the individual person or group, or the community, or society? Is my work effective?

Though imbued with the ideal of achieving social justice for his client and his community, he knows that righteous indignation, religious fervor, and good intentions are no longer enough. He knows he must have knowledge, skill, and the ability to form organizational relationships and mobilize power—in other words, the tools to function in a rapidly changing world. Trying to do the job alone is quixotic and romantic, because the tasks can no longer be accomplished by one person. They must be done in concert with colleagues, with other professions, with principals and interactors in other institutions, in other systems. Nearly every one of the important services by professionals is performed in a complex institutional setting.

As social workers move from discrete social service agencies and highly individualized relationships with clients to institutions where they become professional-technical support to implement policy instead of being the policy-makers themselves, they exert less and less influence. They operate in "worlds they never made." Yet if they believe in equity— the right of all people to have access to beneficial services—they have no choice but to operate in large organizations. This is a hard choice because it is a choice between where they feel comfortable and probably function best, and where the difficult social problems exist and the broader community expects them to contribute.

TWO ISSUES

In order to understand fully the practice dilemmas, the value dilemmas, and the professional dilemmas posed by the ideal of social justice, social workers must understand—and hopefully confront—at least two basic issues. These may be expressed in this way:

1. The enormous difficulty of maintaining *individuality in a mass society*. How can services be provided to large numbers of people without dehumanizing them? The rules, the procedures, the manuals are all necessary, but how can people, the providers as well as the recipients or consumers, remain *persons* despite these essential institutional arrangements, whether in schools, or prisons, or income maintenance organizations, or hospitals?

2. *The need for accountability of professional judgment.* How can the recipients or consumers be protected against error and bias in such judgment? How can professionals measure their effectiveness? How can the community assess the public utility of programs? Intertwined with this knotty problem of accountability is an important assumption that always underlies the social worker's judgment: is the "problem" assumed to be in the person himself or in the social structure? In one case the person's attitude or behavior must be changed; in the other, the system must be changed.

Confronted with these issues, the professional is faced with a series of dilemmas, with judgments and choices he can never escape, operating as he must in large and complex institutions whose goals are oriented to large societal problems. A rational approach to the solution of these problems dictates organizational arrangements such as the division of labor, coordination of effort to achieve commonly held goals, allocation of roles, centralization of accountability, and subservience of the individual to the system. Perhaps the reader will recognize these elements as belonging to the classic description of bureaucracy.

BUREAUCRACY

But bureaucracy cannot be avoided. It is an organizational principle necessary for the stabilization and operation of large and complex social systems. To be sure, the professional person, by his very nature, does not fit into the bureaucratic pattern. What characterizes a professional is inimical to the demands of bureaucratic organization. In a bureaucracy the professional operates in a tension situation; he is constantly trying to reconcile goals, values, and modes of behavior that are different from those he has internalized in professional training. Yet despite the contradictions, professional expertise is required because of the spectacular development of scientific knowledge and its technical application.

Bureaucracy features centralized authority, standardized duties, teamwork, decisions based on rules and regulations, submergence of individual effort, and the product as evidence of success. Professionalism, on the other hand, features collegial relations, individual effort and responsibility based on knowledge and skill, shared responsibility with the client for goal-setting, decisions based on the professional person's individual judgment, and great emphasis on process. Evidence of success relates both to process and product. The dilemma of the professional is having one set of values while working in a place that has another set. The prisons and schools and mental hospitals provide cases in point. They originated as responses to specific situations in specific contexts;

many resulted from genuine reform movements. Gradually they became bureaucracies; otherwise they could not have performed their functions and achieved their goals. When, finally, they incorporated social workers and other professionals into their operations, they produced a classic situation of tension between loyalty to an institution (agency) and loyalty to a superordinate set of values: "the profession." The encouraging feature, however, is that if recognized and understood, this tension can provide a dynamic context for action. The social worker must be constantly aware of this pervasive antagonism. If the awareness does not exist, and if the professional orientation is not protected and cherished, the bureaucracy tends to coopt the professional function and the professional energy to its own purposes. One might note, as an aside, that in struggling with this issue of opposing forces the social worker may be paralleling the struggle experienced by the client in relating to a mass society. Unless the professional can learn to handle his own dilemma, he will probably have difficulty providing help to others.

Ever since the profession came into being, social workers have faced the problem of whether they should work to adjust the system to make it work, or whether to abandon the present arrangements and create a new system. The dilemma has been posed often enough: change the system or provide services within the system. Ideally, the profession should do both. What is unlikely is that an *organization* can do both.

To this writer it appears that within the value structure of the profession, social workers have stated a primary obligation to help people meet their needs. Furthermore, it is legitimate for them to set proximate goals, to refine and reform, and to give energy to making a system work as best it can. In terms of social change they are middle range. Social workers as such have not been creators of social movements; at best they have been middle managers of movements over which they did not exercise control. When they have undertaken more, they have become participants in social movements, rather than managers, and social movements have different protocols for performance and criteria for success.

Can social workers bring about change by withholding or removing themselves from service within existing institutions? No, because they cannot mobilize sufficient power to create alternative arrangements. Difficult as it is (and discouraging), they must find ways to continue the quest to experiment, innovate, reorganize—while continuing to provide services. This writer believes that despite its dysfunctional aspects, bureaucracy is probably the best available way to coordinate large and complex institutions.

So, if one poses the question *How can social workers help maintain individuality in a mass society?* the answers would seem to be: (1) by understanding the tension and conflict; (2) by struggling to handle it;

(3) by not abandoning a currently significant institution or its population; and (4) by continuing to search for new responses to institutional arrangements *while* they serve.

ACCOUNTABILITY

A second fundamental problem involving social work and social justice concerns accountability. In essence, accountability measures goal achievement. What can the individual social worker be held accountable for? Certainly for a definition of the problem. Certainly for identifying the actions that need to be taken. Certainly for taking those actions, and for assessing his actions before reassessing the problem. In short, he can be held accountable for the systematic application of the scientific method as it relates to himself, to his peers, to the consumer of his services, to the sponsors, and to the broader community. But can the community to which he reports hold him responsible for the failure of the institution or the system? For failing to report, yes. For refusing to debate the efficacy of his professional actions, yes. For not subjecting his results to such measurement as is available, yes. But he cannot be blamed for the faults of arrangements he did not create or even have a hand in creating. In most instances, the larger society has accepted social workers when they function as implementers rather than creators of policy. Yet at the same time the finger has been pointed at the profession for not being able to solve social problems. However much they might have wanted it, the truth is that social workers have not had the knowledge or the power or the societal approval to do so. As a result, social work has not had the power and status. It has made the "hard sell," and it has overpromised.

In order to gain adherents social work has promised too much, and when held accountable it has understandably been found wanting. At such times the tendency is to proffer intentions in place of performance. When pressed, a defensive stance develops and with it an avoidance of evaluation and accountability. Once a program (solution) is "found," social workers become carnival barkers selling the program, and are all too reluctant and defensive when it comes to evaluation and accountability. If there were greater acceptance of social work's validity by social workers themselves, there might not be such overpromising. There might be more experimenting, more searching for solutions than selling them. There might even be more acceptance of social work's validity by its various publics.

Accountability—a respectable word that has now entered the jargon— means, by definition, being responsible, being held responsible, being held accountable. But professionals have given it an added connotation that takes it a step further. To them it signifies self-awareness, self-control, self-evaluation. Ultimately, the only effective accountability lies in standards that have been internalized and characterize the actions of the professional person.

This leads to the question of professional standards, for the profession is still far behind in this regard. Criteria must be developed for better ways of developing standards of practice and accountability; for further development and refinement of licensing and renewal of licenses, based on examination and peer review. Experience shows that promotion, advancement, and recognition in large institutions (bureaucracies) tend to be based on the internal needs of the institution, not always on the effectiveness of the service. Large public organizations are usually staffed by civil service administrators, whose orientation tends to supersede those of the social work professionals. The profession has not yet tackled this problem and it should.

In the final analysis, social justice is concerned not just with the equitable distribution of goods and services, but with the right and power of persons and groups to obtain their fair share. Social workers either have assumed or have been assigned special responsibilities on behalf of those who do not get their fair share. Thus social workers necessarily accept as a goal the redistribution of goods, services, and power.

Ultimately it must be recognized that social justice is pursuable, rarely achievable.

6/73—2M—P&K